Utilitarianism: A Very Short Introduction

Very Short Introductions available now:

For more information visit our website

www.oup.com/vsi/

Katarzyna de Lazari-Radek and
Peter Singer

UTILITARIANISM

A Very Short Introduction

OXFORD
UNIVERSITY PRESS

OXFORD
UNIVERSITY PRESS

Great Clarendon Street, Oxford, OX2 6DP,
United Kingdom

Oxford University Press is a department of the University of Oxford.
It furthers the University's objective of excellence in research, scholarship,
and education by publishing worldwide. Oxford is a registered trade mark of
Oxford University Press in the UK and in certain other countries

© Katarzyna de Lazari-Radek and Peter Singer 2017

The moral rights of the authors have been asserted

First edition published in 2017

Impression: 3

Published in the United States of America by Oxford University Press
198 Madison Avenue, New York, NY 10016, United States of America

British Library Cataloguing in Publication Data
Data available

Library of Congress Control Number: 2017932618

ISBN 978-0-19-872879-5

Printed in Great Britain by
Ashford Colour Press Ltd, Gosport, Hampshire

In memory of Derek Parfit

Contents

Preface

Why should the law refuse its protection to any sensitive
being? The time will come when humanity will extend its
mantle over everything which breathes. We have begun by
attending to the condition of slaves; we shall finish by
softening that of all the animals which assist our labors
or supply our wants.

Jeremy Bentham, *Principles of Penal Law*

To destroy a man there should certainly be some better reason
than mere dislike to his Taste, let that dislike be ever so strong.

Jeremy Bentham, arguing against the persecution
of homosexuals

...the principle which regulates the existing social relations
between the two sexes—the legal subordination of one sex to
the other—is wrong itself, and now one of the chief hindrances
to human improvement; ...it ought to be replaced by a
principle of perfect equality, admitting no power or privilege
on the one side, nor disability on the other...

Under whatever conditions, and within whatever limits,
men are admitted to the suffrage, there is not a shadow of
justification for not admitting women under the same.

John Stuart Mill, *The Subjection of Women*

A key feature of utilitarianism is that its proponents have not limited themselves to developing the theoretical basis of their views but instead have strived to bring about practical changes to promote happiness and relieve suffering. They criticized practices that most people accepted as natural and inevitable conditions of human existence. These challenges met with remarkable success.

At a time when there were no laws protecting animals from cruelty, Bentham advocated rights for animals, and his lead was followed later by Mill. Today almost every society has such laws. Bentham was also a great advocate of reforming the dire conditions of prisoners, and of a better system of relief for the poor. The utilitarians advocated broadening the suffrage, to remove the restrictive property qualification, and to extend it to women. They led the campaigns to recognize the rights of women, including allowing married women to own property and to be admitted to university. In all these areas of life, we have transformed our attitudes and practices along the lines that utilitarians sought. Mill was a strong advocate of freedom of thought and expression, and urged that the state should allow individuals to choose their own ways of living, as long as they did not harm others. Bentham's opposition to laws making homosexual acts a crime was far in advance of his times. As we shall see in Chapter 6 of this book, the reforming spirit continues among utilitarians today.

Yet utilitarianism has never lacked opponents. Karl Marx ridiculed Bentham as 'a genius in the way of bourgeois stupidity', whereas Friedrich Nietzsche scornfully refers to utilitarianism—along with Christianity—as a 'slave morality' for 'the cowardly, the timid, the petty'. Among novelists, Fyodor Dostoevsky, Charles Dickens, Elizabeth Gaskell, and Aldous Huxley inserted their opposition to utilitarianism into their fiction. Bernard Williams, a recent British philosopher, concluded a lengthy attack on utilitarianism by remarking: 'The day cannot be too far off in which we hear no more of it.' It is now more than forty years since Williams made that comment, but we continue to hear plenty about utilitarianism. There is, we believe, a very good reason why utilitarianism has outlasted many of its critics, both in the extent to which it continues to have a practical influence, and in the liveliness of ongoing debate about its merits. The fundamental question of ethics is: 'What ought I to do?' and the fundamental question of political philosophy is: 'What ought we, as a society, to do?' To both questions, utilitarianism gives a straightforward answer: that, to put it simply, the right thing to do is to bring about the best consequences, where 'best consequences' means, for all of those affected by our choice, the greatest possible net increase in the surplus of happiness over suffering. That answer covers—at least in principle—every possible situation, and it points to something most of us would agree is worth aiming at. That may be why, as the anti-utilitarian philosopher Philippa Foot once pointed out, utilitarianism does have a remarkable habit of haunting even those who do not believe in it. 'It is as if for ever feel that it must be right, although we insist that it is wrong.'

The statement of utilitarianism that we have just given can be made a little broader, in order to acknowledge that not everyone accepts that the best possible life is the one in which there is the greatest surplus of happiness over suffering. We will discuss the variety of views on this topic later, but for the moment it is enough to modify the statement in the previous paragraph by analysing 'best consequences' in terms of the greatest possible net increase in well-being, however that term is understood, rather than simply happiness. Utilitarianism is then one theory, or better, one set of theories, within the larger family of consequentialist theories. This larger family includes non-utilitarian theories that understand 'best consequences' in ways that are not limited to consequences for well-being.

Utilitarianism pushes us to examine the boundaries of our moral thinking, and consider the interests of those who we often leave out of our concern. It is not surprising that this style of thinking

should sometimes be controversial. We hope that this book
will give you a better understanding of utilitarianism, how it
can be justified, what it takes to be intrinsically valuable, the most
common objections to it (and the best responses to them), the
role that rules can play for utilitarians, and how utilitarianism
is being applied to practical issues today.

Acknowledgements

This book exists because of an invitation from Latha Menon at Oxford University Press. We appreciate Latha's confidence in us and her guidance in planning and writing the book. We also thank Jenny Nugee at OUP and Saraswathi Ethiraju at SPi Global for seeing the book through the production process, Carrie Hickman for assistance with the images, and Edwin Pritchard for his copy-editing, which saved us from some errors.

We are especially grateful to Richard Yetter Chappell, Roger Crisp, and Will MacAskill for reading the manuscript and giving us valuable comments. Fara Dabhiowala provided information on the Bentham quotation on homosexuality, Joshua Greene assisted us with the psychological research we refer to in Chapter 2 and supplied the four 'trolley problem' diagrams used to illustrate that section. Bart Schulz shared his typescript for *The Happiness Philosophers*, which was very useful to us in writing Chapter 1 of this book. Piotr Makuch kindly permitted us to use his photo to illustrate pleasure in Chapter 3.

Katarzyna de Lazari-Radek thanks the Polish National Science Center NCN for financially supporting her work on Chapter 3 (DEC-2013/09/B/HS1/00691).

As we were completing our work on this book in the first days of 2017 we received the grievous news of the sudden death of the most extraordinary philosopher of our times, Derek Parfit. Parfit embodied, to the greatest degree that either of us has known, the true spirit of philosophy: a passion for understanding the deepest questions, combined with a rare gift for formulating new and cogent arguments in a variety of fields. Many of these arguments were supportive of utilitarianism, or more broadly, consequentialism, and critical of non-consequentialist positions. We refer to several of them at various points.

Parfit was not only a philosophical genius, he was also an extraordinarily kind and gentle person who was very generous in sharing his remarkable gifts. In the days after his death, many of his colleagues and former students have recalled how he willingly spent his precious time discussing their work or writing long and detailed comments on their drafts. We ourselves benefited immensely from this in the writing of our first book, *The Point of View of the Universe*. We refrained from asking him to look over the draft of the book you now have before you, because we knew that he was working even harder than usual to complete the third volume of his magnum opus, *On What Matters*. Fortunately this third volume was already in press at the time of his death. The final section, in particular, contains much that is relevant to utilitarianism. A projected fourth volume, on topics more directly relevant to practical ethics, will now never be written. That is a huge loss to philosophy, and to the world. Future discussions of the issues covered in this book will also be the poorer for Parfit's death. Personally, we are already sorely missing him. We dedicate this book to him.

List of illustrations

that comment, but we continue to hear plenty about utilitarianism. There is, we believe, a very good reason why utilitarianism has outlasted many of its critics, both in the extent to which it continues to have a practical influence, and in the liveliness of ongoing debate about its merits. The fundamental question of ethics is: 'What ought I to do?' and the fundamental question of political philosophy is: 'What ought we, as a society, to do?' To both questions, utilitarianism gives a straightforward answer: that, to put it simply, the right thing to do is to bring about the best consequences, where 'best consequences' means, for all of those affected by our choice, the greatest possible net increase in the surplus of happiness over suffering. That answer covers—at least in principle—every possible situation, and it points to something most of us would agree is worth aiming at. That may be why, as the anti-utilitarian philosopher Philippa Foot once pointed out, utilitarianism does have a remarkable habit of haunting even those who do not believe in it. 'It is as if we for ever feel that it must be right, although we insist that it is wrong.'

The statement of utilitarianism that we have just given can be made a little broader, in order to acknowledge that not everyone accepts that the best possible life is the one in which there is the greatest surplus of happiness over suffering. We will discuss the variety of views on this topic later, but for the moment it is enough to modify the statement in the previous paragraph by analysing 'best consequences' in terms of the greatest possible net increase in well-being, however that term is understood, rather than simply happiness. Utilitarianism is then one theory, or better, one set of theories, within the larger family of consequentialist theories. This larger family includes non-utilitarian theories that understand 'best consequences' in ways that are not limited to consequences for well-being.

Utilitarianism pushes us to examine the boundaries of our moral thinking, and consider the interests of those who we often leave out of our concern. It is not surprising that this style of thinking should sometimes be controversial. We hope that this book will give you a better understanding of utilitarianism, how it can be justified, what it takes to be intrinsically valuable, the most common objections to it (and the best responses to them), the role that rules can play for utilitarians, and how utilitarianism is being applied to practical issues today.

Chapter 1
Origins

Ancient precursors

The core precept of utilitarianism is that we should make the world the best place we can. That means that, as far as it is within our power, we should bring about a world in which every individual has the highest possible level of well-being. Although this may seem like mere common sense, it is often in opposition to traditional moralities. Most communities prescribe rules to be followed irrespective of whether the outcome will make the world better or worse. It is much easier to follow rules than to try to assess, each time one acts, which of the available options will have the best consequences. Nevertheless, the key utilitarian insight is so simple and attractive that it is not surprising that thinkers in different times and places have come to it independently.

Mozi, a Chinese philosopher who lived from 490 to 403 BC, in an era known as the Warring States Period, appears to be the earliest person recorded as advocating something like utilitarianism. The dominant ethic of the time was Confucianism, which sees ethics as focused on one's role and relationships, and one's duties are dependent on traditional customs. Against this view, Mozi uses a mode of argument familiar to philosophers today: he tells a story that serves as a counter-example. Mozi imagines a tribe in which the custom is to kill and eat first-born sons; his point is that customs are not self-justifying. We need a standard by which to assess them, and Mozi proposes that the standard should be: does the custom lead to more benefit than harm? Moreover, in evaluating harm, he says, we should not focus only on harm to those with whom we are in a special relationship. Our concern for others, he urges, should be universal. Mozi was a practical person. Not content with condemning the aggressive warfare that prevailed in his time, he sought to deter military aggression by devising better defensive strategies and improving the fortifications of cities so that they could resist sieges.

Mozi lived at about the same time as the Indian thinker Gautama, better known as the Buddha. Buddhist thinking has utilitarian tendencies, for it teaches its followers to reduce suffering—their own and that of others—by cultivating compassion for all sentient beings. A century later, in Greece, Epicurus anticipated the later utilitarians by proposing that pleasure and pain are the proper standard of what is good and bad.

The early utilitarians

In Europe, the idea that we should take the general good as the criterion for right action became popular in the 18th century. One of the first to suggest this was Richard Cumberland, Bishop of Peterborough (1631–1718), whose major work *De legibus naturae* (*On natural laws*) opposed the egoism of Thomas Hobbes and proposed that no action can be morally good 'which does not in its own nature contribute somewhat to the happiness of men'. Lord Shaftesbury (Anthony Ashley Cooper, the third Earl of Shaftesbury, 1671–1713), whose *Characteristics of Men, Manners, Opinions, Times* was very widely read in the years after its publication in 1711, held that the highest form of goodness is 'to study universal good, and to promote the interest of the whole world, as far as lies within our power'. The phrase 'the greatest happiness of the greatest number' first occurs in Francis

Hutcheson's *An Inquiry into the Original of our Ideas of Beauty and Virtue*, published in 1726. In the middle of the 18th century similar wording was used by Claude Adrian Helvetius, a Swiss-French Enlightenment philosopher, and by Cesare Beccaria, an Italian jurist. Jeremy Bentham (1748–1832) read Beccaria and used 'the greatest happiness of the greatest number' as a catchphrase summing up utilitarianism. Bentham says that he was also influenced by the chance reading of a pamphlet by the Unitarian clergyman Joseph Priestley (1733–1804), and by the Scottish philosopher David Hume (1711–76). On reading Hume's demonstration, in his *Treatise of Human Nature*, that whether we regard something as a virtue is determined by its utility, Bentham 'felt as if scales had fallen from my eyes'.

Despite Bentham's central role in the development of utilitarianism, the work that first made the utilitarian view widely known was William Paley's *Moral and Political Philosophy*, published in 1785. Paley, a clergyman, argued that God wants us to promote the happiness of all, and we ought to obey God's will. Among secular utilitarian writings, William Godwin's *Enquiry Concerning Political Justice*, published in 1793, was also, for many years, better known than Bentham's work.

The founder: Bentham

Bentham, the founding father of utilitarianism as a systematic ethical theory and as the basis for reforming society, was a child prodigy (see Figure 1). His father sent him, at the age of 12, to study law at Oxford, but instead of practising law, he returned to London to write about ways of reforming the law. He described himself as a hermit, but he had friends with whom he discussed his ideas, including the Earl of Shelburne, a liberal political figure who briefly became Prime Minister, and James Mill, the father of John Stuart Mill. He also made an extensive trip through Europe to Russia, to visit his brother who was then working as an administrator for Prince Potemkin.

Jeremy Bentham.

1. Jeremy Bentham, the founder of modern utilitarianism.

From 1776, when Bentham first used the 'greatest happiness of the greatest number' formulation of the principle of utilitarianism, he dedicated himself to promoting that objective. (The formulation was, as Bentham later realized, unfortunate because it misleads people into thinking that for utilitarians, something that makes 51 per cent of the population slightly happier would be right, even if it makes 49 per cent utterly miserable.) There is a story that Bentham thought of the name 'utilitarian' in a dream in which he imagined himself 'a founder of a sect; of course a personage of great sanctity and importance. It was called the sect of the *utilitarians.*'

In 1780 Bentham completed his *Introduction to the Principles of Morals and Legislation*, the work in which he most explicitly sets out the theory of utilitarianism. It was not published for another nine years because the book to which it was supposed to be an introduction remained incomplete. That is characteristic of Bentham's writings: sixteen of his books were published during his lifetime, a substantial output for any serious thinker, but one that is dwarfed by the 72,500 manuscript sheets—about 36 million words—that Bentham left unpublished when he died. By 2016, 33 of an expected 80 volumes of the *Collected Works of Jeremy Bentham* had been published. (Transcribe Bentham, an online initiative, makes it possible for anyone able to decipher difficult handwriting to read these manuscripts and, by transcribing them, bring their publication closer.)

Bentham gained international fame for his proposals for the reform of legal systems and of prisons. One of his best-known practical proposals was the 'Panopticon', a design for a prison or factory that would enable prisoners or workers to be observed at any time, without them knowing exactly when they were under observation. Today the Panopticon has a negative connotation because of its systematic denial of privacy, but Bentham saw one of its advantages as enabling the person in charge to ensure that warders or supervisors did not mistreat those under their control.

In the last two decades of his life Bentham put much of his energy into writing an ideal code of law, which he then tried to have implemented. His writings on the codification of law were translated into French and Spanish, and his code was close to being adopted by a liberal Portuguese government when counter-revolutionary forces took over and doomed any chance of reform. Bentham also corresponded with the presidents of the United States, Argentina, and Colombia, all in the hope of seeing his work put into effect, but to no avail.

It is less well known that for much of his life, from the 1770s to the 1820s, Bentham wrote essays and short treatises in defence of sexual freedom. At a time when much lauded thinkers like Dr Samuel Johnson said that 'severe laws, steadily enforced' should be used to prevent the 'evils' of 'irregular intercourse', Bentham pointed out that the pleasures of sex are unusual in that they can be enjoyed equally by the rich and poor, and urged that to allow these pleasures to be maximized, restraints imposed by 'blind prejudice' should be removed. Differences in sexual tastes should not be punished unless they could be shown to cause harm, and such demonstrations were lacking. In various writings Bentham systematically set out and refuted every conventional argument for making homosexual acts a crime. He did not seek to publish any of this work, but instead looked forward to a time, after his death, when publication would become possible. He might have been surprised how long it took—a century and a half—for Western ideas about sex to catch up with his thinking.

When only 21, Bentham wrote a will leaving his body to dissection. The growth of medical science meant that there was a constant shortage of bodies that could be used for research, but at that time dissection was illegal except when carried out on the bodies of executed criminals. Later Bentham decided that his body should, after dissection, be turned into an 'auto-icon' so he left instructions for preserving and exhibiting it. You may still visit Bentham at University College London. His skeleton, dressed in his own clothes, is on public display in a wooden cabinet with a glass front, surmounted by a likeness of his head in wax, because the preservation of the head was unsuccessful. Bentham's will suggested that the case holding his body might be brought out when friends or supporters meet 'for the purpose of commemorating the founder of the greatest happiness system of morals and legislation'. In accordance with this suggestion, the authors of this book had the pleasure of Bentham's company at a dinner celebrating the 200th anniversary of the birth of John Stuart Mill.

The advocate: John Stuart Mill

When James Mill (1773–1836), a Scot who had come to London hoping to make his career as a journalist, met Bentham, Mill's eldest son, John Stuart Mill (1806–73), was 2 years old. James Mill became Bentham's friend, disciple, and an effective popularizer of his ideas, while his precocious child was soon seen as Bentham's intellectual heir. The young Mill never went to school, instead being intensively tutored by his father at home. Like Bentham, he learned a remarkable amount at a very early age, for he tells us in his *Autobiography* that he could read ancient Greek at 3, and Latin at 8. By 15, he had read most of the classics in their original language, knew French, read widely in history, and mastered a considerable body of thought in mathematics, logic, the sciences, and economics. Only then was he introduced to Bentham's work. On reading Bentham he became, as he later wrote, 'a different being. The feeling rushed upon me, that all previous moralists were superseded, and that here indeed was the commencement of a new era in thought.'

During Mill's childhood, his father earned only a very modest income from writing reviews and articles, while devoting much of his time to working on the first history of British rule in India. The publication of that work in 1817, to wide acclaim, transformed the family's fortunes. Though James Mill was critical of much that the British had done in India, he was offered a position with the East India Company, the effective ruler of British India. In 1823 he was able to arrange for his son, then aged 17, to be employed by the company as well. Fortunately for posterity, the work was not so demanding as to impede the younger Mill's learning and writing.

When Mill was 24, he met Harriet Taylor, who was to have a profound influence on his thinking. She was two years younger, but whereas he was single, she was married with children. They became close, so close that some of Mill's friends warned him that he was risking a scandal. He ignored their warnings. Twenty years later, in 1851, two years after the death of Harriet's husband, they married (see Figure 2). Harriet died in 1858, and Mill felt the loss

2. John Stuart Mill and Helen Taylor, Harriet's daughter.

deeply. The following year he published his most celebrated work, *On Liberty*, and dedicated it to her, writing that, along with everything that he had written for many years, 'it belongs as much to her as to me'.

Mill established his reputation as a philosopher with his *System of Logic*, published in 1843, which he followed up five years later with his *Principles of Political Economy*. The works that best represent his contributions to utilitarian thinking, however, came later: *On Liberty*, in 1859, *Utilitarianism*, first published in 1861 as a series of three articles in *Fraser's Magazine*, and *The Subjection of Women*, which appeared in 1869.

There is a debate about whether Mill was consistently utilitarian in all his writings. Some passages of *On Liberty* appear to express a commitment to individual liberty that goes beyond the good consequences that Mill believes liberty brings. Yet Mill's own statement on this issue could not be clearer: 'I forego any advantage which could be derived to my argument from the idea of abstract right, as a thing independent of utility. I regard utility as the ultimate appeal on all ethical questions.' He adds that this must be 'utility in the largest sense, grounded on the permanent interests of man as a progressive being'. When, two years later, in *Utilitarianism*, he states the principle he is setting out to defend, he does so in the straightforward language of classical, or hedonistic, utilitarianism: 'actions are right in proportion as they tend to promote happiness, wrong as they tend to produce the reverse of happiness. By happiness is intended pleasure, and the absence of pain; by unhappiness, pain, and the privation of pleasure.' Nevertheless, even in this work, Mill's eagerness to reconcile utilitarianism with the opinions of his contemporaries raises questions about his fidelity to hedonistic utilitarianism. Perhaps the best-known example, to be discussed in more detail in Chapter 3, is his attempt to show that utilitarianism is not 'a doctrine worthy only of swine', but can justify preferring the 'higher' pleasures of philosophy above the 'lower' pleasures available to pigs.

The impetus that utilitarianism provided for reforms that we now take for granted is nowhere clearer than in Mill's work for the equality of women. Mill, like Bentham, was often critical of institutions based on 'established custom and the general feelings' and that, as he points out in the opening chapter of *The Subjection of Women*, is the only basis for keeping women in a subordinate position. On this issue Harriet Taylor had a major influence on Mill's thinking. She was, by his own account, the primary author of an essay entitled 'The Enfranchisement of Women' published initially over Mill's name in the *Westminster Review* in 1850 and later over their joint names. Although she died fifteen years before *The Subjection of Women* was published, Mill credited her, as well as her daughter Helen Taylor, with many of the ideas expressed in that work.

When Mill wrote *The Subjection of Women*, women could not vote and a married woman was unable to own property or money separately from her husband—indeed, she was, in English law, not a separate legal entity. Mill argues forcefully that this subordinate status is not only wrong in itself, but 'one of the chief hindrances to human improvement'. It ought, Mill wrote, 'to be replaced by a principle of perfect equality, admitting no power or privilege on the one side, nor disability on the other'.

During his short tenure as a member of parliament Mill sought to advance equality for women, along with a variety of other reforms. He moved an amendment to the Reform Act of 1867 to extend the suffrage to women, but it was heavily defeated and it took another sixty years for women to achieve the equal voting rights that his amendment would have brought. His efforts to change the law to allow married women to retain their own property were also unsuccessful, although in that area the law was changed only two years after Mill lost his seat in parliament.

The academic philosopher: Henry Sidgwick

Henry Sidgwick (1838–1900; see Figure 3) entered Trinity
College, Cambridge, as a student in 1855 and remained there
till the end of his life. In 1874 he published his first and most
important book, *The Methods of Ethics*. The depth of Sidgwick's
knowledge of the history of his subject is shown by his *Outlines
of the History of Ethics for English Readers*, published in 1886,
but his interests were not limited to ethics. He also published
The Principles of Political Economy (1883), *The Scope and Method
of Economic Science* (1885), and *The Elements of Politics* (1891).

While writing these other works, Sidgwick continued, for the
remainder of his life, to revise *The Methods*. Five editions
appeared during his lifetime, and he was working on a sixth at the
time of his death. (The now-standard seventh edition corrected a
few clerical errors in the sixth.) Sidgwick's aim was to present and
compare the different 'methods' of reasoning that we use when
we decide what we ought to do. His book discusses three of these
methods: egoism, the view that we ought to aim at our own good;
intuitionism, which prescribes following certain rules no matter
what their consequences; and utilitarianism.

Sidgwick describes himself as greatly influenced on the one hand
by Immanuel Kant's idea of duty and a need for what he called
'one fundamental intuition' that can serve as the basis of ethics;
and on the other by John Stuart Mill's utilitarianism. In contrast
to Mill's *Utilitarianism*, which was written in haste and has been
accused of committing various blatant fallacies, *The Methods* is
notable for the care with which it discusses a wide range of issues.
Among these are objectivity in ethics, the failure of common-sense
morality, the possibility of discerning self-evident moral truths,
the nature of ultimate good, our obligations to the poor, and
whether utilitarians should seek the highest average level of
happiness or the greatest total quantity of it. The fact that Mill's

3. Henry Sidgwick, author of 'the best book ever written on ethics'.

work remains more widely read today is attributable at least in part to the fact that *The Methods* is 500 pages long, and Sidgwick's prose is less fluent than Mill's.

John Rawls described *The Methods of Ethics* as 'the first truly academic work in moral philosophy which undertakes to provide a systematic comparative study of moral conceptions'. This method of comparative study, which has now become standard in philosophical writings, may be Sidgwick's most important contribution to the subject, although his specific views on particular issues remain remarkably relevant to contemporary ethical discussions. J. J. C. Smart, a prominent 20th-century utilitarian, said simply that *The Methods* is 'the best book ever written on ethics'. Derek Parfit agreed with that judgement, acknowledging that some books, like Plato's *Republic* and Aristotle's *Ethics*, are greater achievements, but noting that because Sidgwick could build on the work of his predecessors, *The Methods* 'contains the largest number of true and important claims'.

In 1869 Sidgwick resigned his Trinity College fellowship on the grounds that he could not subscribe to the Thirty-Nine Articles of the Anglican Church. He was made a lecturer, a position that did not require that he attest to his religious faith, and so was able to continue his academic career. His act of honesty gave impetus to the movement against religious tests for university posts, and parliament abolished them two years later. Sidgwick was then able to resume his fellowship. In 1883 he was appointed Knightsbridge Professor of Moral Philosophy, the most prestigious position a moral philosopher can hold at Cambridge University.

Although Sidgwick was far from an orthodox religious believer, he had a strong interest in the possibility of survival after death, not least because reward and punishment in an afterlife could have overcome, for practical purposes, the contradiction between egoism and utilitarianism. Sidgwick was involved in establishing the Society for Psychical Research, founded in 1882 and still in existence, and became its first president. The society sought to test the veracity of those who claim to be able to communicate with the dead. Sidgwick kept an open mind, but was never satisfied that any of these claims were genuine.

Sidgwick paved the way for the eventual admission of women to Cambridge by organizing the first 'Lectures for Ladies' and renting a house in which the ladies attending the lectures could live. This led to the founding of Newnham Hall as a hall of residence for women. It also brought about Sidgwick's marriage, at the age of 38, to Eleanor Balfour, who came to live in Newnham Hall in order to study mathematics, at which she excelled. She later published three papers on electricity, co-authored with Lord Rayleigh, who received the Nobel Prize for Physics. Eleanor's brother, Arthur Balfour, had been one of Sidgwick's students; he later became leader of the Conservative Party and Prime Minister. Eleanor shared Sidgwick's interest in investigations into psychic phenomena, and they worked together to advance the cause of women's education, with Eleanor becoming Principal of Newnham College (as Newnham Hall had become) in 1892. The marriage appears to have been primarily, and perhaps exclusively, a meeting of minds. It produced no children, and there is some evidence to suggest that Sidgwick's romantic feelings were directed towards men.

The 19th century saw utilitarianism develop from Bentham's dogmatic advocacy to Sidgwick's measured and sophisticated philosophy. Over that period, it lost some of its early reforming zeal, but retained significant influence in politics and economics while becoming firmly established as a rational, if still controversial, approach to ethics.

Sidgwick's Trinity College student G. E. Moore (1873–1958) accepted his teacher's view that the right action is that which brings about the best consequences, but denied that only pleasure or happiness are intrinsically good, adding friendship and the appreciation of beauty as independent values. This form of utilitarianism was known then as 'ideal utilitarianism'—today it would be called simply a form of consequentialism. Moore is best known, however, not for his contribution to utilitarianism but rather for the way in which his *Principia ethica* redirected moral philosophy towards a group of new problems that are now regarded as part of 'meta-ethics', a separate branch of the field concerned with the definition of moral terms such as 'good'. For much of the 20th century, the areas of moral philosophy thought to be breaking new ground were in meta-ethics rather than normative issues such as the choice between utilitarianism and its rivals. Philosophers returned to a strong focus on normative and applied ethics only in the 1970s.

Chapter 2
Justification

Bentham on justifying the utilitarian principle

On ethical questions, to express your opinion is not enough; you need to say something that justifies it or is capable of persuading others to accept it. The form that one thinks justification should take will depend on one's views about the nature of ethics itself: that is, about whether moral judgements can be true or false, or are better understood as merely expressions of our attitudes. Proving an ethical first principle is notoriously difficult. Should we try, like Descartes, to come up with a self-evident first principle that can serve as a foundation for all our other ethical judgements? That is the method known as 'foundationalism'. Or do we want to follow the example of John Rawls and use the method of 'reflective equilibrium', justifying ethical principles by how well they match our moral judgements, while also reconsidering the judgements themselves in the light of their coherence with plausible principles?

Bentham has an indirect way of establishing his first principle. In his *Introduction to the Principles of Morals and Legislation*, he asks, of the principle of utility: 'Is it susceptible of any direct proof?' and answers that it is not, for 'that which is used to prove everything else, cannot itself be proved: a chain of proofs must have their commencement somewhere'. Bentham believes that we are naturally inclined to appeal to utility to judge ourselves and others, but confusion and inconsistency may lead someone 'to be disposed not to relish' the principle of utility. He invites those so disposed to ask themselves a series of questions that pose choices, with each choice leading to a further question. The sequence is intended to drive us to the conclusion that all the alternatives to the principle of utility have unacceptable implications. The set of forking paths through which Bentham leads his imagined opponent can be represented by a simplified flow chart (see Figure 4).

Bentham's statement of this argument is extremely compressed—he takes less than a page to dismiss several possible positions, each of which could be the subject of a book. Looking at the left side of the flow chart, someone might say that our likes and dislikes—'sentiments' as Bentham calls them—are the only possible basis for judging right and wrong (as we shall see, the 20th-century Australian philosopher J. J. C. Smart thought this, even though he was a utilitarian). One could also resist Bentham's claim that subjectivism leads to anarchy. That will depend on whether people share a preference for peaceful means of resolving disagreements, rather than resorting to violence. If they do, then they may all agree to set up a democratic political system in order to achieve their common end.

The most serious problems, however, are on the right side of the flow chart. Few philosophers would want to discard the principle of utility entirely, but many would think that it can be overridden by absolute rules—for example, that killing an innocent person is always wrong. If such a set of rules can be defended, that would answer Bentham's question about how the principle of utility can be limited. Alternatively, it might be argued that justice, honesty, or respect for human dignity are independent principles that must, somehow, be balanced against utility.

Finally, the sequence on the right of the chart ends by asking the proponent of a non-utilitarian position what motive there might

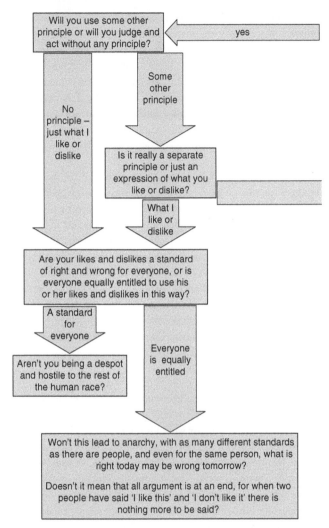

Will you use some other principle or will you judge and act without any principle?

yes

Some other principle

No principle – just what I like or dislike

Is it really a separate principle or just an expression of what you like or dislike?

What I like or dislike

Are your likes and dislikes a standard of right and wrong for everyone, or is everyone equally entitled to use his or her likes and dislikes in this way?

A standard for everyone

Aren't you being a despot and hostile to the rest of the human race?

Everyone is equally entitled

Won't this lead to anarchy, with as many different standards as there are people, and even for the same person, what is right today may be wrong tomorrow?

Doesn't it mean that all argument is at an end, for when two people have said 'I like this' and 'I don't like it' there is nothing more to be said?

4. Bentham's justification of the principle of utility: a simplified flow chart.

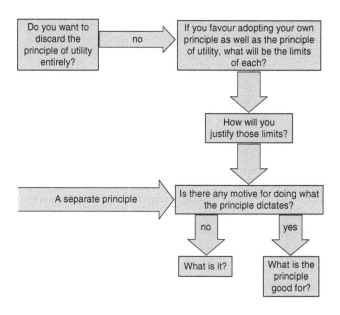

be for acting on it; but here Bentham is in a glasshouse throwing stones. The opening sentence of his *Introduction* reads, 'Nature has placed mankind under the governance of two sovereign masters, *pain* and *pleasure*. It is for them alone to point out what we ought to do, as well as to determine what we shall do.' The most natural reading of this sentence is that it is *our own* pain and pleasure that motivates our actions, for it would be implausible to claim that everyone is always governed by the motivation of trying to reduce pain and increase pleasure for all. So if Bentham questions whether a non-utilitarian principle can be motivating, the challenge can be turned against him: why should the principle of utility be motivating for people who care only about their own pleasure and pain? As we are about to see, John Stuart Mill's attempt to justify the principle of utility raises the same problem, more explicitly.

Mill's proof

Mill's *Utilitarianism* is the second most frequently recommended text in philosophy courses today (only Aristotle's *Ethics* is recommended more often) and of all the justifications that have been offered for utilitarianism, Mill's is undoubtedly the most widely discussed. That doesn't mean that it is the best.

At the start of *Utilitarianism* Mill explains what sort of methodology might be available to decide what is right or wrong. Those who belong to the intuitive school, he explains, believe in 'a natural faculty, a sense or instinct' by which we can know, immediately, as a self-evident truth, what moral principles are to be accepted. Mill himself belongs to the opposing inductive school, which holds that we learn right and wrong from observation and experience. This choice affects the way he tries to justify utilitarianism.

Mill follows Bentham in holding that ultimate ends cannot really be proved, but that this does not mean that we cannot say anything in support of them. Since utilitarianism claims that the only thing that we should aim at is happiness, we can start by asking why we should take happiness as the ultimate end. Mill says that questions about ends are questions about what is desirable. What evidence can we produce that happiness is desirable? Mill's answer is: 'the sole evidence it is possible to produce that anything is desirable, is that people do actually desire it.'

This is not a promising beginning. A drug addict desires heroin, but that doesn't mean that heroin is desirable. 'Desirable' usually carries the sense of 'worthy of being desired' rather than 'able to be desired'. Henry Sidgwick, the third of the trio of great 19th-century utilitarians, thought that Mill's use of the inductive method was an error, for experience 'can at most tell us that all men always do seek pleasure as their ultimate end...it cannot tell us that any one ought so to seek it'. G. E. Moore, at the start of the 20th century, made Mill's derivation of 'good' from 'what is desired' the chief target of his highly influential argument against the 'naturalistic fallacy'—roughly speaking, the fallacy of deriving values from facts.

Mill continues:

> No reason can be given why the general happiness is desirable, except that each person, so far as he believes it to be attainable, desires his own happiness. This, however, being a fact, we have not only all the proof which the case admits of, but all which it is possible to require, that happiness is a good: that each person's happiness is a good to that person, and the general happiness, therefore, a good to the aggregate of all persons.

Here too Mill is on dubious ground. The fact that I desire my own happiness does not mean that I desire the happiness of all. Perhaps I am the kind of nasty character who enjoys making others miserable; or I may just be an egoistic hedonist who is completely indifferent to the happiness of others, and so would prefer a minor increase in my own happiness to a major increase in everyone else's happiness. If many people are like that, can we still say that the general happiness is 'a good to the aggregate of all persons'? That would depend on how we understand this idea. Is Mill saying that because we each desire our own happiness, we must also each desire the general happiness? In private correspondence on this question, Mill denied this; he meant merely to argue, he says, that 'since A's happiness is a good, B's a good, C's a good, etc., the sum of all these goods must be a good'. If this is how we should interpret Mill's claim, however, it makes an unexplained move from the statement that A's happiness is a good *to A* to the claim that it is simply 'a good'. The fact that A desires his own happiness is a description of a state of affairs, whereas to say that something is 'a good' is to make a normative claim. David Hume had already noticed that earlier philosophers made observations about what 'is' and then suddenly drew from them a conclusion about what 'ought' to be; and he pointed to the need to explain how such a conclusion could follow from such premises. Mill offers no such explanation.

When Mill is discussing justice, later in *Utilitarianism*, he quotes Bentham as saying: 'everybody to count for one, nobody for more than one.' He then adds that the principle of utility is 'a mere form of words without rational signification, unless one person's happiness, supposed equal in degree (with the proper allowance made for kind), is counted for exactly as much as another's'. This remark has been interpreted as indicating that Mill assumes that the readers he is addressing are prepared to accept some idea of impartiality as essential to morality; egoism is, for him, not really a contender for the status of moral theory. If this interpretation is correct, it could explain why Mill believes that there is no gap between 'A's happiness is a good for A, B's happiness is a good for B, and so on', and 'the sum of all these is a good to all'.

We can now see why Mill's justification of utilitarianism has been so widely discussed: it is useful for teaching students to spot fallacies in philosophical arguments! Whether the apparent fallacies are real is a question we will leave to serious scholars of Mill's work; but even if we read Mill as charitably as possible, it has to be said that Mill's writing is loose and his meaning often unclear. Sidgwick, the third of the great 19th-century utilitarians, had the advantage of having read both of his predecessors and so was able to avoid some of the problems that he and other critics found in their work.

Sidgwick's proof

Sidgwick opens his major work, *The Methods of Ethics*, by telling his readers that it is not his aim to prove utilitarianism right, but rather to find self-evident, objectively true moral judgements or axioms. By the end of the book, however, it is clear that Sidgwick finds utilitarianism highly plausible, even if he is unable to eliminate egoism as a coherent rival to it.

In contrast to Mill, Sidgwick holds that ultimate ethical principles are truths of reason that we can see to be self-evident, by which he means that these truths are not inferred from any other principles. He does not mean that they are obvious. This makes him a philosophical intuitionist. Intuitionists typically claim that common-sense morality is based on self-evident moral intuitions. Sidgwick devotes a large part of his book to scrutinizing the moral rules that correspond to virtues such as wisdom, self-control, benevolence, justice, good faith, veracity, prudence, and purity, but in contrast to most intuitionists, he concludes that the apparent self-evidence of common-sense morality disappears when we try to apply its rules in particular cases.

Common-sense morality tells us, for example, not to lie. But what exactly does that mean? May we say something that is literally true, but which we know will mislead the person to whom we say it? When my friend asks me what I really think of the tattoo she has just got, must I tell the truth? Is it wrong to please your family by taking part in a religious ceremony that requires you to utter words you do not believe? Is it permissible to lie to a small child about who brings Christmas presents? Or to lie to an older child about whether the illness she has just been diagnosed with is likely to be curable? Common-sense morality does not tell us that we must *never* lie, but as soon as we try to refine its rules so that they will give us some guidance about the exceptions, the clarity and apparent self-evidence of those rules break down. 'Tell the truth except when…' cannot be a self-evident moral truth if the exceptions are not themselves clear and self-evident.

This is just one example from Sidgwick's extensive analysis of common-sense morality, the upshot of which is to suggest that the rules of common-sense morality, with all their qualifications and exceptions, are not self-evident, but require a deeper explanation. That explanation is that they are means of guiding our actions towards the greater good. They are not perfect guides, of course, because they are subject to many kinds of distortion, for instance from selfish interests, superstition, and ignorance. Nevertheless, the utilitarian principle of doing what will bring about the greatest good has explanatory power that no other moral theory possesses.

This idea, that utilitarianism can explain, and therefore help to systematize, our common-sense moral ideas, looks very like Rawls's theory of reflective equilibrium, which we mentioned at the outset of this chapter. But on that model the true moral theory is the one that best explains our common moral judgements. Sidgwick rejects the idea that truth in ethics is constituted by our common moral judgements; instead he seeks truly self-evident moral principles at a higher, more abstract level than the rules of common-sense morality. He proposes four conditions that a self-evident proposition has to meet:

- The terms of the proposition must be clear and precise.
- The self-evidence of the proposition must be ascertained by careful reflection.

- The propositions accepted as self-evident must be mutually consistent.

- To the extent that other equally competent judges deny the truth of a proposition that I hold, my own confidence in the truth of that proposition should be reduced, and if I have no more reason to suspect that the other judges are mistaken than I have to suspect that I am mistaken, this should lead me, at least temporarily, to 'a state of neutrality'.

Sidgwick finds three principles that meet these requirements.

- *Justice* requires us to treat similar cases alike, or as Sidgwick puts it: '... whatever action any of us judges to be right for himself, he implicitly judges to be right for all similar persons in similar circumstances'.

- *Prudence* tells us that we ought to have 'impartial concern for all parts of our conscious life', which means giving equal consideration to all moments of our own existence. We may discount the future because it is uncertain, but 'Hereafter *as such* is to be regarded neither less nor more than Now.'

- *Benevolence*, like prudence, considers the good of the whole, rather than of a mere part, but in this case it is not our own good, but universal good. Hence, Sidgwick says, the principle of benevolence requires us to treat 'the good of any other individual as much as his own, except in so far as he judges it to be less, when impartially viewed, or less certainly knowable or attainable by him'.

This principle of benevolence is, for Sidgwick, the basis for utilitarianism, although for the principle to lead to hedonistic utilitarianism, we still need an argument saying that pleasure or happiness, and nothing else, is intrinsically good. Sidgwick considers that question separately, and we will discuss it in Chapter 3.

A justification of this kind can only be as strong as its foundations. How can we know that they are true? Even with Sidgwick's conditions it is possible to imagine other axioms that would seem self-evident to some people but are inconsistent with the three just described. Sidgwick finds himself unable to deny that egoism can also be based on a claim that appears to be self-evident, namely that 'the distinction between any one individual and any other is real and fundamental, and that consequently "I" am concerned with the quality of my existence as an individual in a sense, fundamentally important, in which I am not concerned with the quality of the existence of other individuals'. Sidgwick recognized that this claim is inconsistent with his own principle of benevolence, and hence leads practical reason to point in two distinct directions. His inability to resolve what he called 'the dualism of practical reason' led him to think that he had failed in his attempt to put morality on a rational basis.

Harsanyi's argument from rational choice under conditions of ignorance

John Harsanyi (1920–2000) was a Hungarian-born economist and mathematician. After a narrow escape from the Holocaust, he again found himself in danger of persecution after the Second World War, this time from the communist regime. He fled to Austria, and then to Australia before eventually settling in the United States. In 1994 his work in game theory was recognized when he shared the Nobel Prize in Economics with John Nash and Reinhard Selten. Harsanyi also applied his expertise in decision theory to ask what principle rational egoists would choose, if they were choosing for a social situation in which they did not know what their own position would be. Harsanyi argued that if they knew only that they had an equal chance of obtaining any of the social positions existing in this situation, from the highest down to the lowest, they would choose to maximize average utility in the society as a whole, because that would maximize their own expected utility. Harsanyi added that this 'equal chance' should apply not only to the objective social and economic conditions in which those choosing might find themselves, but also to their subjective attitudes and tastes, so that they would judge the utility of another individual's position in terms of the attitudes and tastes of the person actually in that position.

Ironically, this device of choosing social principles behind what John Rawls was later to call a 'veil of ignorance' became famous because Rawls drew upon it to argue *against* utilitarianism in his influential *A Theory of Justice*. Rawls denied that rational egoists would, under these conditions, seek to maximize average utility. Instead he proposed that they would choose a principle of equal liberty and a principle of distribution that gives absolute priority to improving the position of the worst off. When we consider objections to utilitarianism in Chapter 4 we will say more about Rawls and priority for those who are worse off. Here we will content ourselves with the comment that the section of *A Theory of Justice* in which Rawls argues that rational egoists behind a veil of ignorance would choose his two principles, instead of maximizing average utility, is one of the weakest in the book.

In a later article, Harsanyi formalized his original argument, showing that what he called 'absolutely inescapable criteria of rationality' for making policy decisions under conditions of uncertainty, combined with a 'hardly controversial' requirement for optimal choice derived from the Italian economist Vilfredo Pareto, 'logically entail utilitarian ethics'. Although it is possible to reject some of the assumptions on which Harsanyi rests his proof, his essay does show that utilitarianism, in some form, can be derived from a limited set of assumptions about maximizing self-interest when uncertainty about the position one will occupy in a society forces one to choose impartially.

Smart's appeal to attitudes and feelings

J. J. C. Smart (1920–2012) was an English-born philosopher who, like Harsanyi, moved to Australia in his early thirties; but Smart, unlike Harsanyi, spent the rest of his life there. In 1961, he published a fifty-page booklet entitled *An Outline of a System of Utilitarian Ethics*. At the time most philosophers rejected the view that moral judgements are statements about something that can be known, or can be true or false; instead, they saw statements like 'We ought to help others when we can' or 'It is wrong to act cruelly towards animals' as expressions of attitudes or feelings. When this view was combined with the belief that philosophy is a matter of reason and argument, the implication was that discussing ultimate ethical principles is not within the scope of philosophy. Smart earns his place in a discussion of how to justify utilitarianism precisely because although he believed that moral judgements are merely expressions of attitudes, he nevertheless found something to say, as a philosopher, about ultimate moral principles. He therefore shows that you can be a utilitarian even if you do not think moral principles are really capable of being justified at all. Because he thinks that a belief in objective truth in ethics is old-fashioned, he sees himself as presenting 'Sidgwick in a modern dress'.

Smart's aim is to state utilitarianism in a persuasive form, rather than to show that it is true. He argues that those who think we should stick with certain moral rules, like 'do not tell lies', no matter what the consequences, need to defend themselves against the charge of heartlessness, for when faced with a choice between obeying a moral rule or preventing unnecessary suffering, they obey the rule. Moreover, once we accept that no moral principles are true or false, these non-utilitarians cannot respond to the charge of heartlessness by saying that we must follow their principles because, heartless or not, they are *true*. If our moral principles express our attitudes and feelings, then when conformity to a rule feels heartless, that feeling is a sufficient basis for us to reject it.

Smart knows that this manner of persuading people to be utilitarians succeeds only when utilitarians are addressing people who share some of their fundamental attitudes. The utilitarian must appeal, Smart tells us, to the sentiment of 'generalized benevolence' which he describes as the disposition 'to seek happiness, or at any rate, in some sense or other, good consequences for all mankind, or perhaps for all sentient beings'. But then, Smart doubts that, in the absence of this sentiment, a discussion of ethical questions could ever be profitable.

Hare's universal prescriptivism

R. M. Hare (1919–2002), who held the chair of moral philosophy at the University of Oxford from 1966 to 1983, shared with Smart and most other moral philosophers of his time the view that moral judgements are not statements that can be true or false. Instead of holding that moral judgements are expressions of attitudes, however, he thought that they are a kind of prescription, the form of speech to which imperatives belong. Prescriptions, even though they do not state facts, are subject to logical rules. 'Shut all the doors' states no fact but it contradicts 'Leave the back door open.' The fact that prescriptions can contradict each other makes it possible to reason about them.

If avoiding contradiction were the only way in which we could reason about morality, no argument for utilitarianism would be possible, for there are many non-contradictory moral theories. To take moral reasoning further, Hare appealed to an idea we have already encountered in Sidgwick's principle of justice. If I say you ought not to cheat on your taxes, then I must also hold that if I am in similar circumstances to you, I ought not to cheat on my taxes. I cannot claim that the cases are different because it is I who benefit when I cheat on my taxes, whereas when you cheat on yours, you benefit. 'I' refers to an individual, and moral judgements must be based on universal properties not on references to individuals.

Like Smart, therefore, Hare could say that he is modernizing Sidgwick. For Hare, this meant reinterpreting his principle of justice as an implication of our use of moral language. Moral judgements, he claimed, must be universalizable. This idea resembles the more familiar Golden Rule: 'Do unto others as you would have them do unto you.' George Bernard Shaw put one objection to the Golden Rule when he quipped: 'Do not do unto others as you would that they should do unto you. Their tastes may not be the same.' Hare's response was that universalizability requires us to do unto others as we would have them do unto us, *if we shared their tastes.*

Universalizability means, according to Hare, that using moral language commits me to a moral judgement about all relevantly similar cases, including hypothetical cases. To discover if I am really able to assent to the judgement that, for example, I ought to tell the truth in a particular situation even though doing so will have bad consequences, I must put myself in the position of all those who would be affected by telling the truth in that situation, and imagine that I am living all of their lives, and this requires me to give the desires and preferences of all those affected by the action as much weight as I give my own. On that view of universalizability, the only moral judgements we can prescribe universally are those that maximally satisfy the desires and preferences of all those affected by our actions. The argument has now led us to utilitarianism, or more specifically, to preference utilitarianism, which differs from the classical hedonistic form in that instead of maximizing happiness or pleasure, it maximizes the satisfaction of desires or preferences.

Both Hare and Smart think it an advantage of their approach that they avoid talk of mysterious self-evident moral truths. Whereas Smart thought that, without such mysterious truths, one must admit that utilitarianism rests on a subjective attitude, Hare thought he could prove that if one is to use moral language at all, the only consistent option is a form of utilitarianism. He argued that the concept of universalizability that is implicit in moral language requires us to give equal weight to the preferences of all those affected by our actions—and requires us to take account of nothing but those preferences.

Can one really maintain that all this is implicit in moral language? We think not. Even if moral language did have the implications that Hare claims for it, his argument would achieve less than one might think, because it would invite those who disagree to invent different terminology which would not have these implications. There is, as Hare admits, no logical requirement to use moral language or to act in accordance with moral reasoning. Hare does not argue that the amoralist is being inconsistent or irrational. Instead Hare appeals to prudential considerations as a reason for not being an amoralist. Whether there always are such prudential reasons against amoralism will depend on individual circumstances.

Despite the differences in the views of the utilitarians we have discussed so far, there is something important that they all share. Consider:

- Bentham's idea, which Mill endorses, that everybody is to count for one and nobody for more than one;
- Sidgwick's requirement that we regard the good of any one individual as equivalent to the good of any other;
- Harsanyi's choice in a position of ignorance that forces us to be impartial between all members of the group for which we are choosing;
- Smart's sentiment of 'generalized benevolence'; and
- Hare's analysis of moral language as requiring us to put ourselves in the position of all of those affected by our actions.

All of these philosophers can be seen as presenting utilitarianism as the best understanding and application of the insight that underlies the Golden Rule. Nor is it an accident, we believe, that something akin to the Golden Rule lies at the core of the ethics of many different cultures and civilizations, from the Jewish and Christian traditions to those of India and China. That utilitarianism can plausibly be seen as an implication of the same insight is a further argument in its favour.

Greene: arguing for utilitarianism by debunking opposing principles

In the 21st century, a new argument for utilitarianism has emerged, based on research in cognitive science about how we make moral decisions. This argument needs to be framed carefully. Many scientists have attempted to deduce values from their account of the facts. Such attempts invariably fail. But Joshua Greene, an experimental psychologist and neuroscientist with a background in philosophy, has shown that it is possible to draw on scientific research in a manner that bolsters the case for utilitarianism while avoiding the fallacy of deducing an 'ought' from an 'is'.

Greene's research began with a pair of imaginary situations known as the trolley problem. In the first case, *Switch*, a runaway trolley is heading down a train track. If you do nothing, it will kill five people. The only thing you can do to save the five is move a switch that will divert it down a side-track, where it will kill one person (see Figure 5). (All the people are strangers, and you don't know any personal details about them.) In the second case, *Footbridge*, there is again a runaway trolley that will kill five people unless you act, but this time you are standing on a footbridge over the tracks and there is no switch. You think about sacrificing your own life by jumping onto the track in front of the trolley, but you realize you are too light to stop it. A stranger wearing a heavy backpack is standing next to you, however, leaning over the rail. The only thing you can do to save the five is push him off the footbridge onto the track in front of the trolley. He will be killed, but the weight of his backpack will stop the trolley before it hits the five (see Figure 6).

Most people respond to these cases by saying that it is permissible to hit the switch, but not to push the stranger. Yet in both cases, you are killing one person to save five. Why then do we react differently to them?

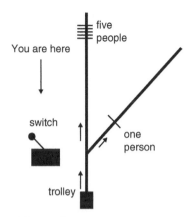

5. The trolley problem: *Switch*.

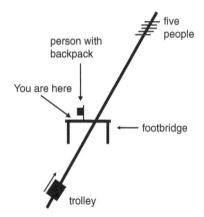

6. The trolley problem: *Footbridge*.

Philosophers have been discussing the trolley problem for many years. One initially plausible response is that in *Switch* the death of the person on the side-track is a foreseen but unintended side-effect of saving the five, whereas in *Footbridge* you intend to kill the stranger as a means to saving the five. But this distinction is difficult to draw—if, miraculously, the stranger you push into the path of the trolley survived the impact but the trolley was stopped, you would be delighted, so in that sense his death is also unintended. Moreover, a third case, *Loop*, shows that the distinction between killing as a side-effect and killing as a means to an end is not decisive in how most people judge the cases. In *Loop*, you can pull a switch to divert the trolley, but this time the side-track loops back onto the main track, where it would still kill the five, were it not for a stranger who is asleep across the tracks. The trolley will hit that person, killing him, but his body will stop it going any further, so the five will live (see Figure 7).

In *Loop*, therefore, as in *Footbridge* the stranger on the track is being used as a means to an end, not as a mere side-effect. Yet most people respond to *Loop* in the same way as *Switch*, and not in the way they respond to *Footbridge*.

Philosophers typically treat the trolley problem as a philosophical puzzle to be solved by producing a theory that will justify our

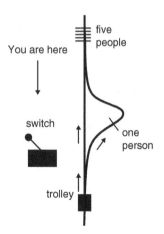

five
people

You are here

switch

one
person

trolley

7. The trolley problem: *Loop*.

apparently conflicting intuitions. Greene wanted to understand why we have these intuitions. He asked people to respond to both *Switch* and *Footbridge* while they were undergoing functional magnetic resonance imaging, allowing him to see which parts of their brain were active while they were answering. Typically, in *Switch*, the regions of the brain associated with cognition were more active, whereas in *Footbridge* the regions associated with emotion were more active. Greene speculates that this was because *Footbridge* involves hands-on physical violence, and *Switch* does not. Over the past decade, research using a variety of different methods has supported not only the specific finding about the trolley cases, but also a general view of moral decision-making that fits within a broader account of how we make many different kinds of decisions. This broader account is known as dual-process theory.

Greene explains dual-process theory by pointing to a device with which many of us are familiar: a camera that has an automatic 'point and shoot' mode, as well as a manual mode. For taking photographs in everyday situations, 'point and shoot' is quick, convenient, and generally gives better results than people with limited time and no special expertise would get by using manual mode. In special circumstances, however, when the light is unusual, or we are trying to achieve a particular effect, we will do better to adjust the settings ourselves, taking time to work out what will give us the best result. Moral thinking, Greene finds, is rather like that. We have very rapid, emotionally based, responses to common situations—we think of them as 'gut reactions' or as a 'yuck' response. In *Footbridge*, for example, most of us have a strong gut reaction against pushing a stranger to his or her death. We don't have to think about it, we just intuit that it is wrong. That reaction is likely to have evolved over the millions of years in which our ancestors lived in small, face-to-face groups that could not tolerate a high-level of intra-group violence. (Violence between groups is a different matter, but is not an everyday occurrence.) On the other hand, we have no similar emotional response to using a switch to divert a trolley. Switches and trolleys are recent inventions that played no role in our evolutionary history. In the absence of any automatic response, we calculate the consequences, and most of us conclude that it is better to save five lives than one.

To test the hypothesis that the application of direct personal force plays a crucial role in our differing moral judgements in *Switch* and *Footbridge*, Greene devised a new situation: *Remote Footbridge* (Figure 8). Once again, there is a runaway trolley and a stranger on a footbridge, but this time you are not on the footbridge. Instead, you are standing next to a switch that will open a trapdoor where the stranger is standing, causing him to fall onto the tracks and be killed, but saving the five.

In *Remote Footbridge*, the proportion of respondents prepared to say that it is permissible to bring about the death of the stranger

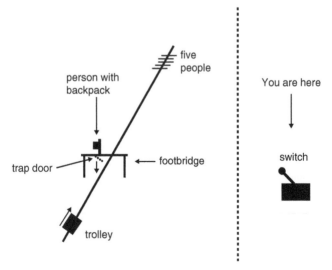

8. The trolley problem: *Remote Footbridge*.

on the footbridge was more than twice as high as it was in *Footbridge* (63 per cent as compared to 31 per cent).

This example shows one way in which scientific evidence can affect our moral judgements. On being presented with *Footbridge*, most people think it would be wrong to push the heavy stranger. On being presented with *Remote Footbridge* (without having first been presented with *Footbridge*), most people think it would be permissible to operate the switch that opens the trapdoor. Now what do *you* think when you reflect on those differing responses? Do you agree that the means by which you ensure that the stranger falls onto the tracks just before the trolley passes under the footbridge makes a crucial difference to whether you did something wrong? If, like us, you think that the means by which you kill the stranger could not possibly make such a difference to the wrongness of killing him, you have made a moral judgement: we ought not to think *both* that it is wrong to push the stranger off the footbridge *and* that it is not wrong to operate the switch to open the trapdoor that will drop him on to the tracks. Given that judgement, and adding the information that many people's judgements in *Footbridge* and *Remote Footbridge* are affected by the use of direct personal force, rather than a switch, we are now in a position to conclude that in judging trolley problem cases, many people react to an irrelevant factor.

What is that irrelevant factor? It could be that people are too sensitive to the use of personal force, or it could be that they are insufficiently sensitive to harming people by moving a switch. Can we decide which of these it is? We already know that some of our judgements are driven by automatic responses and others by the conscious application of moral principles. We might conclude straightaway that those that come from the automatic responses should not be trusted. Greene thinks that would be too hasty. Some of our automatic responses might have, over millennia of trial-and-error, been tested and proven sound. We may do better by relying on them than by relying on our conscious thought processes. This is less likely, however, when we are making moral judgements in situations about which we could not have developed automatic responses over millennia of trial-and-error. Sexual morality, for instance, is an area of conduct that triggers strong automatic responses, none of which originated in an era of reliable contraception. Is it wrong for an adult brother and sister to have sexual intercourse if they use contraception? In many countries, incest between adult siblings is the only voluntary sexual relationship between two mentally competent adults for which you can go to prison. It does not seem that the reason for our hostility to adult sibling incest is based on a considered judgement of the risk of abnormal offspring, for neither the law nor public opinion distinguishes between situations in which there is a possibility of a child being conceived and situations in which there is no such possibility. It seems much more likely that widespread hostility to all forms of incest is an automatic response that developed in an era when sexual intercourse was likely to lead to pregnancy. If so, we should not consider it a reliable guide when applied to adult siblings who use reliable means to prevent pregnancy.

Our intuitive ethical judgements need special scrutiny when we apply them in circumstances that are different from those in which they are likely to have evolved. Even when the circumstances have not changed, however, our automatic responses will sometimes lead us astray. After all, evolution selects for reproductive fitness, not for moral knowledge or for the highest possible level of well-being. Groups that have sanctions against non-reproductive acts like masturbation, oral sex, and homosexual relationships may have higher fertility and faster growth than other groups without those attitudes. That does not mean that these sanctions are morally defensible.

Applying the camera analogy again, it would be reasonable to conclude that we will do best by following our automatic responses, unless we have reasons for thinking that that is not the best thing to do. If we do have such reasons, we should use conscious reasoning to work out what we ought to do.

We still need to ask whether conscious reasoning will lead us to judge that we ought to do what will have the best consequences or to a view that prohibits some actions whatever their consequences. Greene acknowledges that some moral philosophers do a lot of conscious reasoning to defend their non-consequentialist views, but he argues that they are rationalizing intuitions they already have. As we have just seen, there are evolutionary reasons why societies might develop a negative automatic response to masturbation. Kant, Greene argues, shares this response, but as a philosopher with a theory about what makes acts wrong, he has to give a reason for his response. Therefore he says that masturbation is wrong because it is using oneself as a means. Today most people find this laughable. It is hard to believe that Kant would have reached this conclusion independently of the fact that in the Christian culture in which he lived, masturbation was regarded as wrong.

Greene provides evidence that similar forms of 'intuition chasing' are characteristic of much non-consequentialist moral reasoning. When people are asked for their views on punishment, for example, the judgements typically follow a pattern that indicates that retribution, rather than deterrence or reform, is their major motive for punishing. The evidence indicates that people who support more severe, retributive punishments are less likely to engage in reasoning before responding. It is therefore plausible to believe that non-consequentialist philosophers who defend retributivism as a justification for punishment are simply rationalizing their intuitions.

Greene's argument provides a reason for questioning Rawls's reflective equilibrium model for justifying moral theories. Rawls suggests that a moral theory is like a scientific theory, in that it should match the data—in science, the data might be the results of experiments. If we have a very strong theory that explains most, but not all, of the experimental results, we would look harder at those results that do not match the theory, and perhaps discount them on the grounds that there must have been some unknown factor that led to error. In ethics, according to Rawls, the data are our intuitive moral judgements, after we have considered and perhaps revised them in the light of explanations for why some might be unreliable. Here too, the availability of a plausible ethical theory might itself lead us to change our view of some of our intuitive judgements. We may also go back to the theory, and see if it can be revised in a manner that matches more of the considered moral judgements we are not willing to disregard. After further reflection we will in the end achieve an equilibrium between the theory and our considered moral judgements, and that is supposed to be the best possible justification for the theory.

If Greene is right, however, a moral theory should not be judged by whether it matches our intuitions, many of which will be automatic moral responses that are no longer relevant to the situations we face today. At the very least, the model of reflective equilibrium would need to be widened so that it allows us to take into account research that shows which of our moral intuitions have evolved in circumstances that discredit them as sound guides to what we ought to do. We would then, for the purpose of justifying a moral theory, disregard those intuitions. Depending on what intuitions remain unscathed by these findings, however, the difference between reflective equilibrium and foundationalism, the major alternative, will dwindle, and perhaps vanish.

Greene's work clears away the obstacles that have hindered acceptance of consequentialism. Rejecting emotionally based automatic responses, and the rationalizations that philosophers use to support them, leaves consequentialism as the best available option. As Greene puts it: 'The idea that we should try to make things overall better makes moral sense to everyone.'

Still, it might be objected, isn't this idea that consequentialism makes moral sense also an intuition, as Sidgwick believed? If so, isn't it vulnerable to the same kind of debunking critique that Greene employs against other intuitions?

We think it is possible to distinguish the intuitions that Sidgwick argued lead us to utilitarianism from the kind of automatic emotional responses that Greene describes and debunks. At this point we can buttress Greene's case for consequentialism by adding an argument we have defended more fully elsewhere. We have already seen that Sidgwick's principle of universal benevolence requires us to give no more weight to our own interests than we give to the similar interests of everyone else. Such a principle is unlikely to have been selected for by an evolutionary process; on the contrary, it is exactly the kind of principle that you would expect evolution to select *against*, because evolution selects for principles that confer advantages on us, our kin, those with whom we are in reciprocally beneficial relationships, and perhaps other members of our small tribe or social group. The need for reciprocity and trust within our social group may well have led to the evolution of a sense of fairness, but the impetus to extend that sense beyond our own group is unlikely to be an evolved automatic response. It is more likely to require the use of our ability to reason. Our reasoning is, of course, a product of evolution, for it enhances our prospects of surviving and reproducing; but it also brings with it the ability to understand things that have nothing to do with evolutionary fitness, such as the ability to do higher mathematics. Perhaps it also brings with it our ability to see that our own interests are no more significant than those of other beings who can enjoy life as much as we can, and can suffer as much as we can. If this is right, the rational basis of Sidgwick's principle of benevolence is immune from evolutionary debunking arguments, and hence remains standing when these arguments undermine the grounds for accepting non-consequentialist intuitions.

Chapter 3
What should we maximize?

The classical view

Utilitarianism is a form of consequentialism, a theory that tells us that the right act is the one that has the best consequences. But how do we understand 'best consequences'? Bentham, Mill, and Sidgwick were hedonists: that is, they held that the only thing of positive intrinsic value is pleasure or happiness, and the only thing of negative intrinsic value is pain or suffering. To say that suffering is of negative intrinsic value is not to deny that good things can come as a result of suffering. Things that have negative intrinsic value can still have positive instrumental value—a point Nietzsche seems to have missed in his critical comments about utilitarianism. As we saw in Chapter 1, the view that pleasure is the only thing of intrinsic value was not invented by utilitarians; it goes back to Epicurus. The Epicurean tradition continued to be influential in Roman times. Then Christianity became dominant, and for the next 1,500 years, the idea of pleasure as the sole intrinsic good was out of favour.

The view that pleasure is the only intrinsic good has always faced objections. Plato and Aristotle asked whether all pleasures are good, or only those that are 'noble'. Perhaps the best-known objection, dating back to Roman times, is that to regard pleasure as the only intrinsic good is to advocate a doctrine 'worthy only of swine'. Many people find it intuitively plausible that pleasures of a type that can be enjoyed by pigs—the pleasures of eating, or sex, for example—cannot be of the same value as the pleasures we get from reading a literary masterpiece or listening to an opera. Roger Crisp, a contemporary Oxford philosopher who has played a leading role in reviving hedonism, has delved much further down the phylogenetic tree, asking us to imagine we can choose between the life of an immortal oyster, in which we will experience endless, but very limited, pleasures, and the life of the composer Joseph Haydn, who lived only 77 years but had various pleasurable experiences of different intensity. The life of the oyster will, because it is endless, bring a greater total sum of pleasure than Haydn's finite lifespan, but would you choose it?

Mill's response to the 'philosophy of swine' objection was to claim that in assessing pleasures, we should take into account quality as well as quantity. Pleasures are superior in quality, he argued, if 'all or almost all who have experience of both' have such a decided preference for one kind of pleasure that they would not give it up for any quantity of the other pleasure. On this basis he argues that 'It is better to be a human being dissatisfied than a pig satisfied; better to be Socrates dissatisfied than a fool satisfied.'

A lot has been said about Mill's move, most of it critical. The main objection is that if we distinguish between pleasures on the basis of their quality and say, for example, that going to an opera gives us qualitatively better pleasure than watching a football match, we are introducing a value, like being refined, or intellectual, or noble, that is separate from pleasure, so that it is no longer pleasure that we treat as worth maximizing, but something else, or at best, some other value in combination with pleasure. If this is really what Mill is doing, he is abandoning hedonism.

We therefore face a choice. We can treat pleasure as the only intrinsic good, watch the football if we enjoy it more than opera, and forget about refinement and other values. If it should turn out

9. An instance of what hedonists hold is the sole intrinsic value.

that, like pigs, we can maximize pleasure by wallowing in the mud, then bring on the mud! And bring on, too, pushpin, the simple pub game that Bentham said is as good as poetry, if quantities of pleasure are equal. The alternative is to choose the more refined, more intellectual, or nobler goods, but on the grounds that they have an intrinsic value of their own—which means that pleasure is not the only intrinsic good. We will consider views like this when we discuss arguments for a pluralistic form of consequentialism that includes other intrinsic goods, like knowledge, beauty, and truth (see Figure 9).

The experience machine

In 1974 the American philosopher Robert Nozick introduced a novel argument into this debate, intended to show that we value things other than conscious experiences (and therefore, of course, other than pleasure). Here it is:

Suppose there were an experience machine that would give you any experience you desired. Superduper neuropsychologists could stimulate your brain so that you would think and feel you were writing a great novel, or making a friend, or reading an interesting book. All the time you would be floating in a tank, with electrodes attached to your brain. Should you plug into this machine for life, preprogramming your life's desires?

To forestall the objection that plugging into the machine would be a selfish thing to do, Nozick adds that anyone who wants to plug in can do so, and tells us to ignore the problem of who will service the machines if everyone plugs in. Then he asks: 'Would you plug in? What else can matter to us, other than how our lives feel from the inside?'

Nozick assumes that we would not plug in, and draws on this to show that other things matter to us, apart from 'how our lives feel from the inside'. If other things do matter to us, then Mill's argument from the choice of those who have 'experience of both' will not suffice to defend hedonism, because the experience machine could give you the experiences of Socrates as well as those of the pig and the fool. But we would not actually *be* Socrates and our belief that we had encouraged Athenians to examine their lives more thoughtfully would be an illusion. If the only thing that is of intrinsic value is pleasure, this wouldn't matter, for the value of our pleasant experiences will not depend on whether they are based on reality or on electrodes planted in our brain while we are floating in a tank. Yet it seems that we want our life and our achievements to be real. If we want to climb Mt Everest, then we really do want to climb the world's highest peak, and not merely to have the experience of climbing it while floating in a tank, not even if our experience is exactly the same as we would have if we were to climb Mt Everest. Similarly, we want to have friends who like us, not just to have experiences exactly like those we would have if we had friends who liked us.

Many people find Nozick's thought experiment a knock-down objection to hedonism and to any theory that only states of consciousness, or mental states, are of intrinsic value. What are the alternatives?

Preference utilitarianism

Although economics and utilitarianism are both concerned with utility, early 20th-century economists developed an understanding of that concept that is quite distinct from the way in which the classical utilitarians understood it. At the time, economists were eager to establish their discipline as a science, and were troubled by the fact that states of mind like pleasure and pain are not observable or measurable. So economists began to focus on observable behaviour. If I have one dollar, and for that can buy either an apple or an orange, my choice of the orange reveals my preference for the orange and, it is assumed, getting the orange increases my utility more than getting the apple would. If the price of apples and oranges changes, so that my dollar enables me to buy two apples or one orange, and I now buy the two apples, this shows that my utility is increased more by two apples than by one orange. This is not a prediction that I will get more pleasure from the two apples than from the orange. For economists, whether I do or do not get more pleasure from my choice is irrelevant. It is the choice itself that reveals my preference-ordering at the time of the choice, and getting what I prefer constitutes my utility. In addition to making it possible for economics to look more like a science, this new understanding of utility had the additional advantage that it enabled economics to avoid the appearance of paternalism. Economics is not, its defenders could say, involved in telling people what is good for them; rather, it is about giving people more of what they choose.

The economic concept of utility is close to that used in preference utilitarianism, according to which the right action is the one that does most to satisfy, on balance, the preferences of all those affected by our actions. (The two views of utility are not identical, because preference utilitarians are content to speak of things that we cannot observe, like the strength of people's preferences, and so have no need to take observable choices as revealing people's true preferences.) As we saw in Chapter 2, R. M. Hare was led to preference utilitarianism by his concern to avoid what he saw as mysterious claims about objective moral truths; instead, he viewed moral judgements as prescriptions that we are prepared to universalize, and our prescriptions are based on our desires or preferences. Peter Singer, one of the co-authors of this book, was for a time also sufficiently sceptical of the idea of objective moral truths to accept preference utilitarianism as, at least, 'a first base' because it can be reached merely by universalizing decisions that we make about our own desires and preferences.

Unlike hedonism, preference utilitarianism is not vulnerable to the experience machine objection. If I want to climb Mt Everest, the experience machine cannot satisfy my desire; it can only delude me into thinking that I have satisfied my desire, and that isn't what I want. I might, of course, desire only to have an experience identical to the experience I would have if I climbed Mt Everest. But if Nozick is right in assuming that most of us would be reluctant to enter the experience machine, that suggests that most of us want more than experiences. We want our experiences to be real.

Preference utilitarianism is a form of utilitarianism because it seeks to maximize well-being, understood in terms of the maximal satisfaction of our weighted preferences, where the weighting is in accordance with their strength. But although this account of well-being overcomes the problem of the experience machine, it has problems of its own.

Consider an example suggested by Derek Parfit: an Altruistic Drug Pusher makes people addicted to a certain drug because he knows that he will be able to satisfy their intense desire for the drug, which he will supply at no cost for the rest of their lives. The drug brings no pleasure at all, but also does no harm, as long as the desire for it can be met soon after it begins. According to preference utilitarianism the Altruistic Drug Pusher is benefiting the people he has addicted, but who would want to be benefited in that way? To avoid this implication, preference utilitarians may try to limit the desire-satisfaction that counts as benefiting us to the satisfaction of pre-existing desires. But that will give rise to further problems. By giving you a copy of Jane Austen's *Persuasion*, I may create in you a desire to read *Pride and Prejudice*, and it is plausible to think that the fulfilment of that desire does benefit you.

A second puzzle for preference utilitarians is that they seem to be committed to holding that your well-being can be improved by the satisfaction of your desires, even if you do not know that the desires have been satisfied. (This, remember, is why preference utilitarianism is not vulnerable to the experience machine objection; it is not trying to maximize 'satisfaction' in the sense of an experience, but the satisfaction of your desires in the sense in which they are satisfied if what you desire to happen does happen.) Enter another of Parfit's examples: the Stranger on the Train. During your journey, you sit next to a personable stranger who strikes up a conversation, in which she tells you of her life's ambitions and her prospects of success. You take a liking to her and sincerely want her to succeed, but you don't exchange contact details and never see or hear of her again. Suppose that she does succeed in achieving all that, as she told you, she hoped to achieve. Does that mean that *your* life goes better than it would have if she had failed? That is what preference utilitarianism implies, but it seems odd to say that your life goes better even though the stranger's success has no impact at all on your conscious experiences.

Preference utilitarianism does, as we have seen, take account of all present and future desires. But what about past desires? You have a friend who for most of her life has been an atheist. Now, however, she is dying and in her distressed state, she fears going to hell, and asks you to get a priest to administer the last rites. Do you do that, because it is the desire she has now? Or do you take account of the desires she has had all her life—arguably, when she was thinking more clearly than she is now—and refuse to get a priest for her?

A similar question can be asked about the desires of the dead. If you had a desire to have a certain inscription on your tombstone, does it add to your well-being if, after you are dead, that inscription is indeed on your tombstone? We feel that we ought to fulfil such desires for those close to us, but suppose that a historian discovers that an ancient king wanted a particular inscription on his tombstone, and there is at present no such inscription on it. Does the discovery give us any reason to add the inscription now? Intuitively, most of us would probably say no, it does not. If preference utilitarians give that answer, however, they need to explain why they are drawing a distinction between the satisfaction of a desire that occurs when we are alive, but which we never know about (like the desire that the stranger on the train should achieve her ambitions), and the satisfaction of a desire that we never know about because it only happens after we die.

Preference utilitarians may be able to handle these problems without fundamentally transforming their theory—perhaps they can just accept the implications of their view in each of these cases, implausible as they may seem. A more basic problem concerns desires that you would not have if you were fully informed and thinking clearly. The dying atheist's desire to have a priest administer the last rites is one example. Or perhaps you now want revenge on someone who you believe has deliberately cheated you, but if you were fully informed, you would know that your belief is false, and this person's actions have been misrepresented to you. Assume that you will never discover your mistake, and so if you harm him, you will never regret having done so. If you succeed in harming him, does that make you better off, because your desire has been satisfied? (Put aside the felt sense of satisfaction—we are, again, speaking here only of satisfaction in the sense that what you desire to happen, has happened.)

Some preference utilitarians have sought to answer this objection by shifting from seeing well-being in terms of the satisfaction of whatever preferences you may happen to have, to the view that well-being consists in the satisfaction of the desires we would have if we were fully informed and thinking clearly about all the different actions open to us, and the impact each of them would have on the fulfilment of our desires, both present and future. On this view, if you want revenge on James because you falsely believe that James wronged you, your desire for revenge is not to be counted. Similarly, if you are dying and want absolution from a priest in order to increase your prospects of going to heaven rather than hell after you die, but in fact there is no life after death, then this desire does not count because if you were fully informed you would cease to have it.

If we count only the desires we would have if we were fully informed and thinking clearly, we can disregard all kinds of desires that people have when they are ill informed, or confused, or thinking too hastily. The switch to fully informed desires does, however, transform what seemed at first to be quite a simple view into something extremely complicated. Suppose that Maria is a religious believer, but the truth is that there is no god, so if Maria were fully informed, she would be an atheist. Her chief desires are to do what god wants her to do, and apart from that, to enjoy her life as much as possible. Does this mean that when you want to benefit her, you should ignore all of her religiously grounded desires? Suppose, for example, you know that Maria wants you to wake her in time to go to Sunday mass, which she wishes to attend because she believes that god wants her to do so. You also know that there is no god, and that on this beautiful spring morning, Maria will enjoy herself much more if, having woken too late to get to mass on time, she works in her garden rather than going to church. Those who hold the 'fully informed desire' version of preference utilitarianism would then have to say that you ought not to wake her in time for mass. More generally, they will hold that it is right for you to do things to Maria that are contrary to her most firmly held actual wishes. Moreover, since (we shall assume) Maria will never accept that there is no god, she will, until the day she dies, resent what you are doing to her. Never mind, the preference utilitarian will say, you are doing what Maria would want, if only she were fully informed. Suddenly preference utilitarianism, which seemed at first to be less paternalistic than hedonistic utilitarianism, has lost that advantage.

A different response to the problem of desires based on false information is to say that the desires to which we should give weight are the underlying ones, not those that are conditional on certain facts being the case. For example, in the case in which you desire to harm James because you believe he wronged you, this is merely a conditional desire—you want to harm James, on condition that he did harm you. If he did not, then your underlying desire, which is to act with goodwill to all those who act with goodwill towards you, would prevail. This view seems less paternalistic than the fully informed desire view, because we count your actual, underlying desires, rather than merely hypothetical ones that you would have under certain conditions which are not actual. Nevertheless, in many situations—for example, that of religious believers like Maria—it leads to the same conclusions as the fully informed desire view, and so is just as paternalistic.

A further and perhaps ultimately more serious difficulty arises when we consider desires that seem simply crazy. An example is someone whose greatest desire is to count the number of blades of grass in a lawn. He is not under any illusions about what will happen if he succeeds in accurately completing this task. He just wants to do it. Should we give that desire as much weight as any other similarly strong desire?

Some preference utilitarians are prepared to accept that conclusion, and give as much intrinsic weight to the desire of the grass counter as they would give to, say, a similarly strong desire to avoid severe pain. Others, like John Harsanyi, thought differently. 'It would be absurd', he wrote, 'to assert that we have the same moral obligation to help other people in satisfying their utterly unreasonable wants as we have to help them in satisfying their very reasonable desires.' But if preference utilitarianism is restricted to taking into account only 'reasonable' preferences, it risks ceasing to be a desire-based theory at all. For if, as many philosophers have argued, a reasonable person can see that some things are objectively good, then preference utilitarianism has become a theory that takes into account only preferences for what is objectively good, and so becomes a different type of theory altogether.

Pluralist consequentialism

Preference utilitarianism survives the experience machine objection but has turned out to have serious problems of its own. One way of overcoming these problems makes it converge with theories that claim that we can use our reason to decide what is objectively good. A theory based on a view of what is objectively good could also withstand the experience machine objection, as long as what is taken to be objectively good is not limited to states of consciousness.

Alongside hedonistic utilitarianism and preference utilitarianism, there is a third option, one that used to be known as 'ideal utilitarianism' but is now more often labelled 'pluralist consequentialism'. Pluralist consequentialists want to maximize intrinsic good, but unlike hedonistic utilitarians they do not think that pleasure or happiness is the only thing that is intrinsically good. There are other ideals or intrinsic values, they say, like knowledge, truth, beauty, justice, equality, and freedom. Unlike preference utilitarians, pluralist consequentialists hold that such things have intrinsic value irrespective of our preferences. Some pluralist consequentialists regard these values as part of our well-being—for example, they think that our lives will go better if we have more knowledge, or freedom, even if we do not desire knowledge or freedom, or care about them in any way, and they do not make us happier. Those who take this view are utilitarians, as we are using that term, since they are concerned to maximize well-being. Other pluralist consequentialists hold that some things are of intrinsic value even if they do not increase anyone's well-being. This group can be further divided into those who think that all intrinsic value derives in some way from the existence of conscious beings, even if it does not necessarily conduce to their well-being; and those who think that there can be intrinsic value even in the absence of any sentient beings at all.

Consider first the view that a person's well-being can be increased by something of intrinsic value even if the person does not care about it in any way. To assess this claim we need to be clear about what it is to assert that something is an intrinsic value. It is sometimes said that intrinsic values like knowledge, truth, and freedom are elements of everyone's well-being because even if you are at first indifferent to such values, if you adopt them you will in time be able to appreciate what you have got and, as a result, live a happier life. To argue in this way, however, would not establish that knowledge, truth, and freedom are *intrinsically* good for you; it would only show that they are instrumentally good because they increase happiness.

Can we, for example, regard freedom as intrinsically good, independently of its instrumental value in promoting happiness or the satisfaction of our desires? In *On Liberty* John Stuart Mill presented a classic argument for freedom of expression and for allowing people to choose their own ways of living, as long as they do not harm others. Mill's text is sometimes cited as defending the intrinsic value of liberty. Mill's contention that 'the free development of individuality is one of the leading essentials of well-being' may seem to support the idea that freedom is a component of well-being independently of its contribution to happiness. If, however, we read it in conjunction with Mill's statement that he regards utility as the ultimate test of all ethical questions, and with his account of utility in terms of happiness or pleasure, it is more plausible that he sees freedom as important because it is an essential requirement for individual happiness. In general, we find it difficult to understand how something can be part of our well-being if it does not lead to pleasure, or to other states of consciousness that we like to have, or satisfy some of our preferences or desires. We therefore reject the view that our well-being can be increased by something to which we are, and always will be, indifferent.

That still leaves the possibility of a form of pluralist consequentialism that regards some things other than well-being as having intrinsic value. Such a view has some obvious strengths. It is immune to the experience machine objection, for it can hold that there is intrinsic value in living in reality, without illusions, and in striving to achieve something with one's life. Pluralist consequentialism is, in fact, open to whatever values you think, on reflection, are intrinsically worthwhile. That does mean, of course, that different people will come up with different lists of intrinsic values. A partial list of goods that philosophers have held to be of intrinsic value includes: life, consciousness, health, pleasure, happiness, satisfaction, accomplishment, play, truth, knowledge, rationality, wisdom, practical reasonableness, beauty, aesthetic experience, virtue, religion, communion with god, love, friendship, justice, equality, freedom, peace, and honour. Such pluralistic accounts face an obvious problem: on what basis was one value included and another omitted? Why is this value on the list and not that one?

The answer cannot be: because they all contribute to some other ultimate good. Then that ultimate good would be the sole intrinsic good, and the other values would be instrumentally valuable. This would no longer be a pluralist view of intrinsic good. Alternatively, a pluralist could answer that we must draw on our intuitions to decide what is of intrinsic value and what is not. If this seems unsatisfactory, the pluralist can respond that whether one is a pluralist or a monist (i.e. someone who holds that there is only one intrinsic value), there are no grounds for choosing intrinsic values other than an appeal to one's own intuitions.

A monist may concede that claim, but point to an additional problem that pluralists must face: what are we to do when intrinsic values conflict? In many situations, if we are pluralists, we will often have to choose between different possible actions, each of which leads to an outcome that achieves a different balance between intrinsic values. If there is no basis, other than our own intuitions, for choosing what is of intrinsic value, it would seem that such choices must also be a matter of intuition.

Suppose that we think truth is an intrinsic value: if our grandma gives us a Christmas present that is not at all to our taste, and then asks us how we like it, how do we balance the value of truth with the value of not hurting her feelings? Perhaps in that case we will think of the lie as minor, and allow our concern for grandma's happiness to trump truth; but will we take the same view in more serious situations? Imagine, for instance, that grandma becomes critically ill, and although she is fully conscious now, her doctor tells us that he expects her soon to lapse into unconsciousness, from which she will not recover. She asks us why her son has not come to see her. The truth is that he was on his way to see her, but the plane he is on has disappeared, and seems likely to have crashed. If truth is a value, there would be some value, in these circumstances, to telling grandma this terrible news. Pluralists can, of course, say that this value is outweighed by the inconsolable grief that it would cause, but how do they reach this decision? What would they say to someone who thought the value of truth outweighs grandma's grief? Presumably, only that their intuitions are different.

Similar questions arise for pluralists at the level of public policy, where the appeal to intuitions seems even more unsatisfactory. If we think that freedom is an intrinsic value, should we allow people to drive without seat-belts, knowing that this will increase the road toll? If there is only one intrinsic value, like well-being, these problems are difficult, but in principle we could solve them, if only we could get all the facts. For pluralists they seem to be insoluble.

Classical utilitarians think that pluralists have got themselves into this difficulty because they are victims of an illusion. Just as Sidgwick sought to explain the rules of common-sense morality as rough guides to promoting the greater good, so utilitarians can explain that we value goods like knowledge, justice, equality, and freedom because they promote the greater good. Societies in which these goods are respected and promoted tend to have much greater well-being than societies in which they are not. If, however, we regarded these principles as merely instrumentally valuable, we, and our governments, would be too ready to sacrifice them for minor, short-term, and perhaps self-interested, expediency. It is therefore better that we regard them as intrinsically valuable. So utilitarianism can provide an explanation of our intuition that such goods are intrinsically valuable at the same time as explaining why we should not trust these intuitions, and should instead regard the value of these goods as instrumental, not intrinsic.

Value beyond sentient beings

All of the values mentioned in the section 'Pluralist consequentialism' require the existence of conscious beings. If there were no conscious beings in the universe, and never would be, would anything have value? Would it matter what the universe was like, and what happened in it? Could there be good or bad consequences at all—would the concepts of good and bad even make sense—if there were no conscious beings that would experience those outcomes?

G. E. Moore famously claimed that a beautiful world is better than an ugly one, even if there are no beings who can see or appreciate it. In support of this view, he asked the reader to compare two worlds: one as beautiful as we can imagine it, and the other just 'one heap of filth'. Moore urged that if we make this comparison, we can recognize that it is better that the beautiful world should exist, rather than the ugly one. There is, however, an obvious difficulty in assessing this claim: we are supposed to be reaching a judgement on the basis that there are no beings capable of being affected by the beauty or the ugliness of these worlds, but we are also being asked to imagine them, and in doing so we are being affected by them. It is very difficult to be confident that our judgement of the two worlds is not contaminated by the attitudes we have in imagining them. Your authors, to the extent that we can put aside those attitudes, cease to have any confidence in Moore's intuition that it is better that the beautiful world should exist. What difference does it make, if there is not, and never will be, a conscious being to whom it can make a difference?

Moore himself later came to think that he had made a mistake, and that nothing is intrinsically good unless it has some relation to consciousness. In the 20th century, a new challenge to this view emerged. Some environmentalists hold that there is intrinsic value in preserving wilderness, or biodiversity, and that the importance of preservation does not depend on our appreciation of it, or on other possible benefits we or other animals may gain from it. We can understand the attractions of this view. To drive a species into extinction seems wrong, whether we lose a beautiful, iconic animal like the tiger, or the less appealing Delhi Sands flower-loving fly (the first insect to be protected under the United States Endangered Species Act). This judgement also seems to be independent of the suffering that individual members of the threatened species may experience, because it also seems wrong to bring about the extinction of rare plants. Moreover, we are much more concerned about the deaths of individuals of an endangered species, such as whooping cranes, than we are about individuals of a similar, but not endangered, species like sandhill cranes, although the suffering of the cranes is presumably similar. This suggests that our concern is not for the individual animals, but for ourselves, or for future generations of humans, who will enjoy seeing such animals. As a ground for protecting biodiversity and opposing extinction, this makes sense. To bring about the extinction of a species that has evolved over millions of years and, once extinct, can never be brought back again, is a form of vandalism, akin to the destruction of ancient statues and temples by the Taliban in Afghanistan and Islamic State in Iraq and Syria. It deprives future generations of what should have been part of their heritage. This, however, is not to assign intrinsic value to biodiversity (or to ancient works of art). They are of instrumental value because of their potential to benefit sentient beings, human or non-human, present or future.

Intrinsic value: the story so far

Our reluctance to enter the experience machine counts strongly against hedonism. Preference utilitarianism faces a number of problems, in particular the choice between including all preferences, no matter how ill informed or crazy they may be, or restricting the preferences that are to be counted to those that are well informed and reasonable. Both of these options lead to difficulties. Pluralist consequentialism seems attractive, but are knowledge, freedom, beauty, truth, or biodiversity really valuable in themselves, beyond their value as means to happier or better lives for sentient beings?

Given that every view about what we ought to maximize has serious problems, it is worth reassessing the experience machine argument against hedonism. The argument relies heavily on our intuitions and it is important to consider what factors lie behind our reluctance to be plugged into the machine. Does our intuitive response come from our desire that our experiences reflect the reality of what we are doing and how we are living? Or is it influenced by macabre images from science fiction movies? Perhaps in responding to the example we are not—despite the assurance that everyone can plug in—able to put aside our concern for the rest of the world, and our desire to contribute to making it better. Or maybe we do not trust technology and worry that the supercomputer running the machine will crash, leaving us to wake and face the messy reality we thought we had left forever. Our refusal to enter the experience machine might also be explained by our reluctance to leave behind those we love.

Another possible factor is our strong desire to be 'masters of our own fate' and to have control over our lives. We want to believe that our future depends on who we are, what we do, and what we decide upon. It is possible that such beliefs help us to lead a happy and fulfilled life. We want to have this control even in situations when it must be an illusion. For example, people prefer to choose their own ticket in a lottery, rather than to have a ticket assigned to them, and will even refuse to trade a ticket they have chosen for one with better prospects of winning. Most people believe that a car accident is less likely to happen if they are drivers rather than passengers. Psychologists call this phenomenon 'control illusion' and have been working on understanding it for the last four decades. Herbert Lefcourt, an American psychologist, suggested that 'the sense of control, the illusion that one can exercise personal choice, has a definite and a positive role in sustaining life'. We should not be surprised, therefore, that we have a strong preference not to be in a machine that we cannot control.

A further psychological characteristic that makes us hesitate about cases like the experience machine is our preference for what is real rather than fake. We would be disappointed if our 'diamond' earrings were brilliant fakes even if we will never sell them. We want our handbags to be made by the company of the designer whose label is on them, and when we go to the Louvre, we do not want to be looking at reproductions, no matter how good they may be. We seem to put a lot of importance on genuineness even if we are not sufficiently expert to be able to tell the difference between the genuine and the fake. If it became known that the Mona Lisa hanging in the Louvre is a perfectly made copy that only experts can distinguish from Leonardo's painting, the crowds around it would rapidly thin. Is it rational to put so much weight on authenticity? What does it say about us as rational beings? Why should it be so important that my handbag is the product of a famous designer? If I like the painting why should it matter so much that it was done by the hand of Leonardo? If your *belief* that something is real brings you greater happiness or pleasure, then it is sufficient for you to believe that it is real, whether or not it really is. If you feel so good wearing those earrings because you believe that the stones sparkling beneath your ears are genuine diamonds, isn't that enough? In this respect the experience machine is like a perfect forger, and our desire for more than a perfect forgery is, no doubt, a product of our evolution, but not a preference that we can rationally defend.

If we told you right now that your belief that you are reading this book is an illusion, because you are already plugged into the experience machine, and everything you can remember, including your family and all your friends, has been an illusion, would you want to unplug? A series of experiments indicates that most people would be reluctant to leave the life they are living now, whether it is real or a computer-programmed illusion. It seems that our reluctance to enter the experience machine is affected, like many other decisions we make, by a 'status quo bias'. We like what we are used to and it is an extra effort—and risky—to make a change. So it is no surprise that we do not want to leave the world we know and plug into a machine, especially as we are not sure if it will even work properly. If we were already in the experience machine, however, we may think that leaving it would not be such a great idea either.

If any of the factors we have mentioned plays a significant role in our rejection of the experience machine, then the example does not provide reliable evidence that we want more than the best states of consciousness that we can have. In that case, to the question 'What should we maximize?' the classical utilitarian answer—'pleasure'—remains defensible.

What is pleasure?

Whether pleasure is the only intrinsic value, as hedonistic utilitarians hold, or one of several intrinsic values, as some pluralist consequentialists hold, we need to say more about what it is and how it is related to happiness, with which it is often identified.

You feel pleasure when you are watching an amusing film, reading a gripping book, solving a crossword puzzle, taking part in a lively and enlightening philosophical argument, having a delicious meal or exciting sex, surfing a wave, or riding a bike downhill on a beautiful sunny day. What makes all these different experiences pleasure? Is there anything that they have in common?

On this question, there are two different positions you can take. One is that there is nothing these different experiences have in common except that, at the time of experiencing them, and considering them purely as mental states, we desire them to continue. Admittedly, the feeling of pleasure may be accompanied by other feelings like shame or stress, but if we can separate these different feelings from the feeling of pleasure, we know that pleasure is something we desire for its own sake. On this view, what makes all these varied feelings come under the general term 'pleasure' is our attitude towards them. The other possible position is that different kinds of pleasure have a common 'feeling tone' that accompanies our experiences and makes them pleasurable. Roger Crisp defends this latter view.

Both of these understandings of the nature of pleasures have their pros and cons. The most appealing aspect of the attitudinal view is that it neatly resolves the puzzle of what all the different experiences we regard as pleasurable have in common. If we ask why we call honey, ripe strawberries, and chocolate sweet, we reply that they all share a common taste. In contrast, when we reflect on the diverse experiences we call pleasant, we may fail to find any distinctive feeling that they have in common. That makes the 'feeling tone' view less plausible. On the attitudinal view, it is just the fact that, considering them qua experience or state of mind, we desire them and wish them to continue. This in turn connects pleasure with an attractive understanding of what it is for something to contribute to our well-being. Pleasure necessarily contributes to our well-being (other things being equal) because it is something we want and are motivated to get. That is just what the attitudinal view implies. If we did not want it, considered as a state of consciousness, it would not be pleasure.

On the other hand the feeling tone view is more in accord with current thinking in neuroscience, which treats wanting something and finding it pleasant as two distinct processes, even when what we want is a sensation or state of consciousness. The majority view of neuroscientists has changed since 1954, when J. Olds and P. Milner implanted electrodes into rats' brains and allowed the rats to press a lever that sent an electric current to parts of their brains believed to be responsible for pleasure. The rats pressed the lever thousands of times, even to the point of starving themselves to death. The initial interpretation was that the rats were getting so much pleasure that they neglected everything else. Further research, conducted on humans as well as rats, showed that it is more likely that the stimulation created a desire rather than a feeling of pleasure. It now seems that motivation can be separated from pleasure and if this is right, we should not make the distinctive feature of the state of mind we call pleasure the fact that we desire it to continue. Neuroscientists working on pleasure have described it as 'an additional niceness gloss painted upon the sensation'. That sounds a lot like a distinctive 'feeling tone'.

Whatever our understanding of pleasure is, we can ask whether it is equivalent to happiness, as the classical utilitarians took it to be. They often write as if our happiness can be made up of a long sequence of minor pleasures such as biting into a fresh juicy apple or going for a stroll on a sunny day. Is that right, or do such things leave our happiness untouched? When social scientists seek to measure the happiness of a group of people, they often ask them how satisfied they are with their life. This ties happiness to people's subjective judgements about their lives as a whole: the more positive that judgement is, the happier they are. Life satisfaction may have little correlation with pleasure. People sometimes give positive answers to questions about life satisfaction, while admitting that they seldom have pleasurable experiences.

Happiness is different from pleasure, as it focuses not on a sensation or sequence of experiences but rather on a psychological condition, orientation, or disposition. We might understand it as a positive emotional evaluation, whether of a moment, a day, or the whole of your life. It has been described as a disposition to be in a good mood, to be cheerful, to have a generally positive outlook on life, and so on. It would seem that a disposition can only be valuable, however, because of whatever it is a disposition towards. Consider, for example, the disposition to help people in need—this is a very good thing because it leads to people in need being helped, and if it did not, it would not be of value in itself. If, therefore, we understand happiness as a disposition, it is not happiness itself that is of intrinsic value, but rather the positive feelings that it is a disposition to have.

There are many more questions that studies of happiness seek to investigate. To what extent does raising people's material standard of living increase their happiness? Does the phenomenon of hedonic adaptation—also known as the hedonic treadmill—mean that once people can meet their basic needs, further increases in their material standard of living will have little impact on their happiness? For a utilitarian, all of these questions are important. If we are to maximize good in the world, we need to know both what that good is, and how to bring about more of it.

Chapter 4
Objections

Does utilitarianism tell us to act immorally?

In *The Brothers Karamazov*, Fyodor Dostoevsky has Ivan challenge his brother Alyosha:

> 'Imagine that you are creating a fabric of human destiny with the object of making men happy in the end, giving them peace and rest at last, but that it was essential and inevitable to torture to death only one tiny creature—that baby beating its breast with its fist, for instance—and to found that edifice on its unavenged tears, would you consent to be the architect on those conditions? Tell me, and tell the truth.'

Ivan's challenge has become a famous objection to utilitarianism. Setting out the structure of Dostoevsky's objection more formally may help to clarify what is at issue:

> Premise 1. If utilitarianism were true, it would tell us, correctly, which acts are right and which are wrong.

> Premise 2. Utilitarianism tells us that if torturing an innocent child to death would bring about better consequences than anything else we could do, then torturing an innocent child to death would be the right thing to do.

> Premise 3. Torturing an innocent child to death is always wrong.

Therefore:

> Conclusion: utilitarianism is false.

This basic structure applies to many objections to utilitarianism, with variations in the content referred to in the second and third premises. Utilitarians, or at least those who are willing to speak of moral judgements, and the theories that imply them, as true or false, will accept the first premise, and cannot deny that if all the premises are true, then the conclusion follows. (Utilitarians who do not think truth or falsity applies to moral judgements will need to restate the argument in terms of what they approve or disapprove of, rather than in terms of what is true.) Hence a defence of utilitarianism will require denying either that utilitarianism tells us to do the act in question (rejecting the second premise) or denying that the act in question is always wrong (rejecting the third premise). We will postpone for Chapter 5 one important strategy for rejecting the second premise, namely, modifying utilitarianism so that individual acts are not directly assessed by their consequences, but rather by whether they conform to a moral rule, the general observance of which has the best consequences. In this chapter, therefore, we are asking whether the standard form of utilitarianism, as defined in our preface, can meet the objections pressed against it.

In *The Brothers Karamazov* Alyosha succumbs meekly to Ivan's challenge, replying softly: 'No, I wouldn't consent.' The novel would have had more philosophical tension if Alyosha had shown more resistance. Then the dialogue might have gone like this:

> *Ivan:* Imagine that you are creating a fabric of human destiny with the object of making men happy in the end, giving them peace and rest at last, but that it was essential and inevitable to torture to death only one tiny creature—that baby beating its breast with its fist, for instance—and to found that edifice

on its unavenged tears, would you consent to be the architect on those conditions? Tell me, and tell the truth.

ALYOSHA: But Ivan, I don't understand. How could torturing that baby bring about the peaceful and happy world you describe? You must explain that to me, because otherwise you are asking me to imagine something impossible! And you know very well that in the world in which you and I live, torturing a child is not going to do any good at all. It can only cause pain and suffering and death, so of course it is wrong to do it.

IVAN: It's a hypothetical example. I don't have to explain how torturing the child might really bring about a better world. Just try to imagine that it would.

ALYOSHA: Dear Ivan, if your question has nothing to do with the world in which we live, then my answer will also have nothing to do with this world. So I will answer: Yes, I would consent to be the architect of that wonderful world of universal peace and happiness under the conditions you describe. Just remember, though: my answer has *no* implications for what it would be right to do in the real world.

IVAN: Alyosha, what are you saying? Surely you agree that torturing a child to death—an innocent child, like that baby over there—is always wrong! I simply don't believe that you could do such a thing.

ALYOSHA: You are probably right when you say that I could not do it. I am, as you well know, a gentle person. My dispositions, my empathy with small children, the way I shrink from any violent acts, have been formed in a world in which violence does harm, and in this world, these dispositions serve me well, and also serve well all those around me, including you, my dear brother. That is why we cultivate and praise kindliness, and encourage everyone to react with horror at the idea of torture, and especially the torture of a child. I shudder even to think of such an act! But you did not ask me if I *could* do it. You asked me if, under the hypothetical conditions you specified—which I still cannot imagine in any realistic form—I would *consent* to being the architect of the utopia you described. I took that to be another way of asking if I thought it would be *right* to do it. And even if my deepest nature recoils from the very thought of torturing a child and the depths of my soul cry out against so horrid a deed, nevertheless, under those hypothetical conditions which—do not misunderstand me, Ivan—have *nothing* in common with the real world in which we live, breathe, love, and act, I do believe that it would be right to do it.

Alyosha's responses are convincing. It's not surprising that we who have had our intuitive responses formed in the real world should be repelled by acts that, in a very different world, would have the best consequences. That repulsion is not sufficient reason to think that those acts would still be wrong in an imaginary world in which the good they do undeniably outweighs the bad.

Ivan makes no attempt to show that torturing a child ever could, in the real world, have the consequences that he describes. Some philosophers have suggested more feasible examples that are still troubling for utilitarians. H. J. McCloskey, writing in 1957 when lynchings still occurred in the American South, imagined a sheriff in a town after a white woman had been raped. An angry white mob is ready to attack African Americans, and will probably lynch several of them. If the sheriff were to frame an African American, the mob would lynch him and only one innocent life would be lost. That, McCloskey said, is what a utilitarian would be committed to doing—and McCloskey thought it would clearly be wrong for the sheriff to do it.

A more contemporary version of a similar dilemma asks us to suppose that a surgeon is about to perform a delicate operation on a patient. She learns that there are four patients in the hospital who will soon die if they do not receive an organ—one needs a heart, another a liver, and two need a kidney. The patient she is about to operate on would be a perfect donor for all four of them. The surgeon is capable of performing the delicate operation successfully, but if the patient died, no one would be surprised, or would think the death required investigation. Should the surgeon perform the operation in such a way that the patient dies, so that his organs can save four lives?

In both of these cases—in contrast to the case Ivan put to Alyosha—we can understand how the action that is contrary to our usual understanding of what is right would save lives. But a utilitarian contemplating framing or killing an innocent person would need to have a high level of confidence about all the relevant facts, and in practice that degree of confidence would be difficult to justify. How would the sheriff know that the rapist would not subsequently confess and reveal that an innocent person had been framed? Could the surgeon really be sure that the very convenient death of her patient would not arouse suspicion? Will the transplants succeed, and is there really no other way of saving the lives of those patients? In both situations, public knowledge that a person in a position of trust had, in the most serious way possible, violated the duties and expectations of his or her role could have wider harmful ramifications. If the racist white majority in the town cease to trust the sheriff, they are more likely to resort to the lynch mob as a means of ensuring what they see as 'justice'. If patients learn that surgeons may kill them in order to benefit others, they will stay away from hospitals and probably some will die as a result. So even a small risk of being found out would be enough to tilt the balance against a sheriff framing an innocent person or a surgeon killing a patient.

In terms of the argument structure set out at the beginning of this chapter, the utilitarian strategy here is not to deny Premise 2 outright. Utilitarians cannot maintain that there are *no* conceivable circumstances in which it would ever be right for a sheriff to frame an innocent person, or for a surgeon to intentionally kill a patient who would otherwise make a good recovery. Instead, utilitarians can argue that these circumstances are unlikely ever to occur. If, contrary to expectations, we do find ourselves in those circumstances, then the utilitarian will challenge Premise 3 and maintain that the action would not be wrong. If it conflicts with our intuitions, that is because our intuitions evolved to respond to circumstances we are more likely to encounter. Recall Greene's camera analogy (from Chapter 2): our intuitions are the point-and-shoot mode; our utilitarian judgement in special circumstances is the manual override—and these hypothetical situations are very special indeed.

That response will not satisfy those who think that some actions are so plainly wrong that they must never be contemplated. Elizabeth Anscombe, an English moral philosopher, Roman Catholic, and implacable opponent of utilitarianism who died in 2001, wrote: '...if someone really thinks, *in advance*, that it is open to question whether such an action as procuring the judicial execution of the innocent should be quite excluded from consideration—I do not want to argue with him; he shows a corrupt mind.' Anscombe had her own reasons for holding that it is always wrong intentionally to take an innocent human life, but as a philosopher, she cannot draw on her religious convictions to defend her ethical views. Perhaps that is why she offers no argument, and instead appeals to intuitions that she assumes we share. We may well share them, but, as we have seen, the existence of these intuitions can be explained in a manner that does not give us any reason to think that they are reliable indicators of true or justifiable moral principles.

Measuring utility

If utilitarianism tells us to do what will have the best outcome, and if 'best outcome' means the greatest possible surplus of happiness over misery, or of pleasure over pain, then it seems that we need to be able to measure quantities of these mental states. But even if we focus just on one person—say, I am thinking only about myself—I can't measure my happiness today, and say that

I was 2.6 times as happy today as I was on the same day last year. Making interpersonal comparisons of utility is harder still. Next weekend I could go for a hike with my spouse, which would help to keep us fit and healthy, as well as being an enjoyable day for the two of us, or I could visit my elderly grandmother, which would cheer her up a lot, as she is lonely. Which will do most to increase utility? How can we tell?

Social policy decisions raise similar problems. Suppose that a change to public transport schedules will make 90 per cent of the population slightly happier, but 10 per cent much less happy. Should it have our support? A complete answer to that question would require some way of estimating whether the reduction in well-being of the 10 per cent is more than 9 times greater than the increase in well-being of the 90 per cent. We don't have any way of making such comparisons.

The quest for a means of measuring happiness is not new. In 1881 F. Y. Edgeworth, a student of Sidgwick who made significant contributions to economics, published *Mathematical Psychics*, in which he envisaged a hedonimeter—a device that would measure the intensity of pleasure that a person was experiencing. To make these measurements useful a unit of measurement would be needed. Edgeworth thought that such a unit could be found in the following manner. Suppose that we are comparing two different pleasures, A and B, and we judge them to be equally pleasant, so we have no preference between them. If Pleasure A is then increased to the point at which we can just discern a difference between it and Pleasure B, we can then say that it has increased by one unit of pleasure. Thus the unit of measurement is a 'just perceivable increment' of pleasure. Edgeworth argued that for any given individual, this would be constant over time. He then made the even bolder suggestion that 'Any just perceivable pleasure-increment experienced by any sentient at any time has the same value.' Once that is accepted, Edgeworth thought the rest is merely a matter of arithmetic, multiplying the number of increments by the number of sentient beings affected, in order to determine whether an act or policy is right or wrong.

For more than a century after Edgeworth imagined his hedonimeter, the task of measuring happiness was abandoned as impracticable. Recently, however, interest in it has revived. Daniel Kahneman, a psychologist who won the Nobel Prize in Economics for challenging that discipline's assumptions about human rationality, has enrolled volunteers in a study that requires them, at random intervals, to enter into their mobile phone a number on a scale that rates how positive their experience is at that particular moment. The data can be used to compare how happy an individual, say Emma, is at different times, but it does not give us any basis for saying that when Emma enters the highest number on the scale, she is happier than Miki, who rates her experience as only slightly above the middle point of the scale. We may take these numbers as evidence that Emma is as happy as she has ever been, whereas Miki has been much happier than she is now. Nevertheless, just as a small bottle when full may hold less than a larger bottle that is half-empty, so Miki's capacity for happiness may far surpass Emma's, and the state of mind she rates near the middle of the scale could be happier than the state of mind Emma rates at the top of the scale.

Health economists have used a different measure to compare the benefits of health care interventions, and to offer guidance on which interventions should be funded from national health care budgets. The unit of measurement most commonly used in this field is the quality-adjusted life-year, or QALY. The idea here is that one good achieved by health care is a longer life, but a year confined to bed is not as good as a year in normal health. To find out how much less good it is, researchers have asked people to imagine themselves with various impairments to their health, and then asked them how many years of life they would give up in order to have that impairment cured. Suppose you are a quadriplegic with a life expectancy of twenty years. A physician offers you a new treatment

that will restore you to normal health and mobility, but will reduce
your life expectancy to five years. You think it over and decide not to
have the treatment. Then the physician returns: new research
shows that your life expectancy after treatment will be fifteen years.
You agree to have the treatment. What, we might ask, was your
break-even point, that is, the point at which you would have had no
clear view about whether or not to have the treatment? Let's say,
just to make the maths simple, that it was a life expectancy of ten
years. That implies that you would be willing to give up half of your
life expectancy, but not more, to have your quadriplegia cured and
therefore that you regard a year of life as a quadriplegic as
worth only 0.5 of a year of life in normal health. Whatever your
break-even point may have been, it enables the researchers to
compare the value of very different things, like extending life and
overcoming quadriplegia. In contrast to Kahneman's scale, QALYs
can be added, subtracted, multiplied, and divided. They still do not
tell us if one person's year of life in good health brings her as much
well-being or happiness as the next person's, but for policy planning
purposes it is assumed that, as Bentham put it, 'Every individual in
the country tells for one; no individual for more than one.'

The evidence on which QALYs are based is open to challenge.
If, for example, we want to know how to evaluate life with
quadriplegia, should we be inviting members of the general public
to imagine that they are quadriplegics, and then ask them how
they would trade off life expectancy for a cure? Or should we be
asking people with quadriplegia, and if so, should we be asking
people who have only recently become quadriplegics, or long-term
quadriplegics? Healthy people may well have a distorted idea of
what life would be like if they were confined to bed, but it is
also possible that long-term quadriplegics have adjusted their
expectations of life downwards and forgotten how much better life
was before they had the condition. Nevertheless, given that we
cannot avoid making resource allocation decisions, using QALYs
seems better than abandoning the attempt to measure the benefits
gained through different health care procedures. That, in any case,

is the view of government bodies such as the United Kingdom's National Institute for Health and Care Excellence, which uses QALYs in making recommendations on the allocation of health care resources.

Whether we shall ever be able to make interpersonal comparisons of utility is unclear. For the first time, thanks to progress in neuroscience, we can now observe activity in the brain that reveals whether someone is experiencing pleasure or pain, but even if we become able to correlate more precisely brain activity with the intensity of the pleasure or pain that the subject is experiencing, we will still not know whether similar brain states are experienced by different people as similarly intense pleasures or pains.

If we do not yet have a way of measuring utility, however, that problem is not limited to utilitarians. Other moral theories may lay down rules we must obey, but the rules invariably leave areas of our conduct undetermined. Everyone, utilitarian or not, has to make decisions in which the happiness or unhappiness of those affected by our choice is a factor that it would be wrong to ignore. In these circumstances, we often attempt to make rough estimates of the likely impact of our decisions. How much will grandma mind if we don't visit her this weekend? Will we feel bad all week because we never got the fresh air, exercise, and sense of achievement that we would have got if we had gone hiking? Utilitarians, like anyone else, will sometimes get the answer wrong, but if they make a genuine effort to gather whatever relevant information is available, and on the basis of that evidence, try to reach the best judgement they can, they should not be blamed if that judgement turns out to be wrong.

Bentham himself recognized that we cannot always perform the calculations that strict adherence to utilitarianism would require. 'It is not to be expected', he wrote about the process of summing up the costs and benefits of a particular policy, 'that this process should be strictly pursued previously to every moral judgement, or to every legislative or judicial operation.' We should, he thought, keep it in view, and the nearer we get to it, the more exact our judgement will be.

Despite the undoubted difficulties in measuring utility, there are many situations in which it is clear enough which action can be expected to have the best consequences. Often in these situations we will maximize utility by doing what conventional moral rules would tell us to do anyway. If someone asks me how to get to the nearest train station, and I know the answer, I will very likely maximize utility by providing her with the information she is seeking, rather than by not responding at all, or by lying to her. Normally helping people will do more good than harming them. In other areas, however, as we shall see when we look at applications of utilitarianism in Chapter 6, utilitarians are on firm ground in challenging conventional moral rules.

Is utilitarianism too demanding?

Traditional moralities are usually based on a set of moral rules that tells us what we should not do: we should not kill, we should not steal, we should not lie, etc. In everyday life, it is not particularly difficult to follow such rules, and we are likely to believe that as long as we don't violate the moral rules, we are doing everything that we are ethically required to do. Utilitarianism, in contrast, does not regard a life lived in accordance with such negative rules as fulfilling the demands of morality. The principle of utility requires us to do what will have the best consequences. How we can best do that will vary according to our circumstances, but if we are spending money on luxuries when others are in dire poverty, it would seem that we ought to help them, and it is hard to find a limit on how much help we should give, until we reach the point at which if we gave more, we would be harming ourselves as much as we would be benefiting those we were helping. Such a morality seems extremely demanding.

Here's an example. You live in London, it's February, you are tired of the damp grey weather, and you see an advertisement for winter vacations in Morocco. You'd enjoy that, but first you check how much good your money could do. The Life You Can Save, an organization that recommends cost-effective charities that help people in need in developing countries, has a website with an impact calculator. You enter the cost of your vacation, and select some charities. You learn that for the cost of a week in the sun, you could protect 600 people from malaria for an average of three years, or save the sight of 40 people who would otherwise go blind. Taking the vacation will not do as much good as donating to one of those charities, so utilitarianism says that you can't justify your winter break. By the same standards, many other items that people spend money on without much thought, from dinner at a gourmet restaurant to buying new clothes just because you would like a different look, are not going to be permissible either. And it isn't just money: instead of spending so much time chatting with your friends, shouldn't you be volunteering for an organization that is doing good?

Can morality really be as demanding as that? Or does it make utilitarianism, as some have claimed, a morality for saints rather than for human beings?

Utilitarians can seek to soften the rigour of their theory. Without holidays we would be less efficient in our work. If we try to do good all the time, without breaks to relax and do things with friends and family, we will risk burning out, and therefore, in the long run, doing less good. So perhaps we don't have to be quite as hard on ourselves as it first seemed; but nevertheless, if we are honest, most of us will admit that we are not doing as much good as we could.

Utilitarians could also give a more hard-line response: they could deny that the demandingness of a theory is a reason for rejecting it. Demandingness is not a feature of a moral theory in itself, but of a moral theory applied to beings with a particular nature, in a world with particular features. In a world of isolated tribal communities without extremes of wealth and poverty, utilitarianism will not be highly demanding. In a world with many affluent people who are enjoying a wide range of luxury goods, as well as many people living in extreme poverty, and with effective channels through which the affluent can assist the poor, utilitarianism is more demanding. Even then, if all or most of the affluent were donating a small proportion of their resources to helping people in extreme poverty, utilitarianism would not be highly demanding, because the most important needs of people in extreme poverty would have been met, and it would be less clear whether further transfers increased overall utility. It is only because relatively few affluent people are doing anything significant to assist people in extreme poverty that utilitarianism becomes, for those who are prepared to follow its guidance, highly demanding. Add further facts about the greenhouse gas emissions of the fossil-fuel energy and meat-based diet on which most affluent people rely and utilitarianism becomes more demanding still (but then so would any plausible ethic).

Given that affluent people today live in a world in which utilitarianism is highly demanding, and that very few of them are saints, most of them will not be living up to their obligations. The conventional response to a failure to live up to one's obligations is blame, with the expectation that those blamed will feel guilty for not doing what they ought to do. Utilitarianism, though, takes a different approach to praise and blame. The key to the utilitarian approach is that 'what ought we to do?' and 'what ought we to praise or blame people for doing?' are distinct questions. To praise or blame someone is an act, and so subject to evaluation on the basis of its consequences. Suppose a friend gives 10 per cent of her income to charities, taking care to select highly effective ones; but you know that she could give more, and do more good, if she bought fewer and less expensive clothes. Should you blame her for not doing as much good as she could? In a society in which very few people give anywhere near 10 per cent of their income to charity, that would surely be counter-productive. She will only feel discouraged, and others who give little or nothing will not be encouraged to give if they learn that someone who gives 10 per cent is still being blamed for not giving more. We want to raise the standard for ethical living in our society, and praising people who are giving well above that standard is one way to do that.

Praise and blame come in different degrees, and we can vary our praise and blame in proportion to how far above or below the current standard people are. Why not, then, do the same, not just for praise and blame, but for all the ethical judgements that utilitarians make? Wouldn't it be more fitting for utilitarians to acknowledge that in ethics, we do not have a simple choice between right and wrong, but rather, a spectrum of choices, some of which are better than others? This view is known as 'scalar utilitarianism', a term coined by the philosopher Alastair Norcross. It is suggested by the wording of John Stuart Mill's definition of utilitarianism, according to which actions are right 'in proportion as they tend to promote happiness, wrong as they tend to produce the reverse of happiness'. Until relatively recently, however, no one paid much attention to the suggestion in this definition that actions can be 'more right' or 'less right'.

The scalar view applies neatly to the issue of how much we should do for people in extreme poverty, because we can gradually increase what we give, and it is paradoxical to say that at some point, by giving a penny more, we cease to act wrongly and are now doing what is right. Perhaps we should abandon the notions of right and wrong, or of obligations we either meet or fail to meet, and instead say that our actions steadily get better as we increase our giving? It is true that the idea that an action is either right or wrong fits better with a morality based on obedience to rules than it does with one based on maximizing intrinsic value. Nevertheless, the concepts of right and wrong are so deeply embedded in the way we think about ethics that it would be difficult to abandon them. Given that we can at least partially resolve the problem by the use of praise and blame, it isn't clear to us that it is worth attempting a more radical revision.

Does utilitarianism ignore our special obligations?

Three children have been swept into the ocean by a freak wave. I can see two of them to my left. I am a strong swimmer and could rescue them both. The third child is to my right. If I rescue her, the other two will drown. Rescuing the two, rather than the one, is the way to maximize utility. But the one is my daughter. If utilitarianism tells me that I ought to save the others and let my daughter drown, isn't it ignoring the special obligations that parents have to their children? If utilitarians are always going to maximize the good, impartially viewed, then they are going to be defective as parents, spouses, and friends.

William Godwin, the author of *Enquiry Concerning Political Justice*, and a contemporary of Jeremy Bentham, is one of the few utilitarians to have defended the view that maximizing utility takes precedence over close family relationships. In a famous passage Godwin imagines that he can rescue only one of two people trapped in a burning building: Archbishop Fénelon (a celebrated author of the late 17th and early 18th century) or his chambermaid. Godwin insists that he ought to rescue Fénelon because by doing so he would be helping thousands who have been cured of 'error, vice and consequent unhappiness' by reading his work. Godwin then continues:

> Supposing the chambermaid had been my wife, my mother or my benefactor. That would not alter the truth of the proposition. The life of Fénelon would still be more valuable than that of the chambermaid; and justice—pure, unadulterated justice—would still have preferred that which was most valuable. Justice would have taught me to save the life of Fénelon at the expense of the other. What magic is there in the pronoun 'my' to overturn the decisions of everlasting truth?

Godwin was heavily criticized for this stance, and he himself became more accepting of partiality as a result of his relationship with Mary Wollstonecraft (which was cut short by her tragic death after giving birth to their daughter, Mary Wollstonecraft Shelley, later the author of *Frankenstein*). Such attachments, he wrote, in addition to being a source of our own happiness, help to kindle our own sensibilities and are likely to make us 'more prompt in the service of strangers and the public'. Once we enter into such a relationship, 'it is impossible we should not feel the strongest interest for those persons whom we know most intimately, and whose welfare and sympathies are united to our own'. These benefits outweigh, Godwin suggests, the fact that people in a close relationship will find it impossible to be impartial between the one they love and a stranger.

Something similar can be said about other loving relationships, whether between parents and their children, between other family members, or between close friends. There is ample evidence that children are more likely to thrive in a close and loving family, so utilitarians have good reasons to encourage parents to be warm and loving to their children. Children, as they mature, will naturally reciprocate such feelings, and siblings and close friends will also be partial to each other. For most people, such relationships are a necessary part of a good life. Derek Parfit has described acts of excessive partiality that occur in the course of such relationships as 'blameless wrongdoing'. The acts are wrong, but the motivation of the people doing them is a necessary concomitant of the love that comes with these close relationships, and we do not want to discourage people from forming close relationships. Utilitarians should not, therefore, blame those who have these motives and act accordingly. At the same time, utilitarians can admire the rare people who, in order to do more good to strangers, try to overcome their partiality to their own children. Paul Farmer, the co-founder of the organization Partners in Health, is one of these people. A Harvard medical graduate who could have had a comfortable life treating affluent patients in the

United States, he instead ran a health clinic for the rural poor in Haiti. After he married and had a child, he was disturbed because he realized that he loved his own child more than he loved the children he was treating. Tracy Kidder, Farmer's biographer, suggested that some people would be critical of him for even thinking that he can love the children of others as much as he loves his own child. 'Look,' Farmer replied, 'all the great religious traditions of the world say, "Love thy neighbor as thyself." My answer is, I'm sorry, I can't, but I'm gonna keep on trying.' To avoid forgetting about children other than his own, Farmer carries with him a picture of his daughter and a picture of a Haitian child of about the same age, one of his patients who suffers from malnutrition. This attitude has enabled Farmer to do far more good than he could have done if he were more focused on doing what is best for his own child. If Farmer, because he had come to love his child so much, abandoned his work with Partners in Health, that would have been the wrong thing to do, even though we should not have blamed him for doing it.

Ignoring 'the separateness of persons'

In *A Theory of Justice*, Rawls writes that 'the most natural way' of arriving at utilitarianism 'is to adopt for society as a whole the principle of rational choice for one man'. For one person, it is rational to accept some pain now in order to prevent greater pain later. But, Rawls thinks, utilitarians transfer this idea to society as a whole, believing that it is justifiable to inflict some pain on one person in order to prevent another person experiencing greater pain. This, Rawls believes, is a mistake. It shows that 'Utilitarianism does not take seriously the distinction between persons.' This has now become a stock objection to utilitarianism; but what is it supposed to mean? As we saw in Chapter 2, Sidgwick considered his work a failure precisely because he could not deny that the distinction between individuals is 'real and fundamental', and as a result he was unable to refute egoism. In what way was he not taking this distinction seriously?

Utilitarians hold that it is justifiable to inflict a cost on one individual in order to benefit others, but they don't argue that this is true *because* it is rational for one individual to choose lesser suffering now over greater suffering later. These are separate claims, and many people, both utilitarians and non-utilitarians, hold them both. Anyone who supports taxing people on high incomes and using the revenue to provide benefits to others in need must agree that it is sometimes justifiable to impose a cost on one person to benefit another. The fact that we are distinct individuals is one thing; the rightness or wrongness of imposing costs and benefits on distinct individuals is another.

The objection might also be understood as directed against the idea that individuals are, to utilitarians, mere receptacles of pleasure and pain, and have no significance beyond the value that they can hold. If this were how utilitarians thought, the only thing that would concern them would be maximizing the total net surplus of utility. The death of one individual would not matter, as long as the value she contained could be transferred without loss to another individual. But utilitarians do not need to, and should not, think of happiness as if it were something that could exist independently of individuals, or be valuable apart from its value to individuals. Happiness is valuable precisely because it is good for individuals. Utilitarians can and should value each sentient being as a distinct individual subject of experiences. There is therefore something to be regretted when an individual dies or suffers, even if the upshot of that death or suffering is a greater total amount of happiness, and hence better for individuals on the whole. The 'separateness of persons' objection is therefore an objection to one way in which some utilitarians may have thought about value, but this way of thinking about value is misguided, and not an implication of utilitarianism itself.

We could also understand the objection as saying that once we take seriously the separateness of persons, we cannot add up the sum of the good or bad things that may happen to each of them.

This relates to the problem of interpersonal comparisons of utility, which we have already discussed, but it is not a reason for rejecting all aggregations of costs and benefits between separate people. Parfit refutes that view by asking us to imagine that we are searching for survivors in a building that collapsed in an earthquake. We find two people, A and B, trapped in the rubble, unconscious but alive. The only way to rescue both A and B is to push aside a piece of concrete that will then fall across B's toe, breaking it. If we don't do this, we can rescue B, who will be unharmed, but A will die. Those who hold that it is never justifiable to impose costs on one person to benefit another must say that we have to leave A to die, but surely that is not the right conclusion to draw. The fact that individuals are distinct does not prevent us from weighing up the costs and benefits of our actions to different individuals.

The final variation on the 'separateness of persons' objection that we will consider draws on Kant's claim that it is always wrong to use one person as a means to benefiting another. On the basis of this principle, a Kantian could accept pushing aside the concrete that will fall on B's toe because the harm done to B is an unintended side-effect of rescuing A, and not a means to that end. But suppose that the only way to move the concrete is to ram it with the unconscious B's foot, with such force that B's toe will break. Then we are using B as a means to rescuing A; but given that otherwise A will die, and B will only suffer a broken toe, we still don't think it would be wrong to use B in this way.

The distribution of utility

Imagine that there are only three individuals in the world, A, B, and C, and only two possible distributions of utility:

(1) A: 5 units; B: 5 units; C: 5 units.
(2) A: 15 units; B: 1 unit; C: 0 units.

Utilitarianism favours the second distribution because the total sum of utility is greater. Some think that this constitutes an objection to utilitarianism. Does it? If we think of the units that are distributed as money, we have good reason to prefer 1 over 2. Imagine that each unit represents $1,000. In general, it seems that the more money someone has, the less utility she gets out of each additional dollar. So the chances are good that taking $1,000 from A and giving it to C would decrease A's utility only slightly, while increasing C's greatly. But because the figures in the distributions above represent utility, rather than income or other material means to increasing one's utility, this 'law of diminishing marginal utility' as it is known must have already been taken into account in reaching these figures. We must assume, therefore, that taking one unit of utility from A and giving it to C would decrease A's utility as much as it would raise C's utility. For the same reason, we should not reject the second distribution on the grounds that the figures fail to take account of the envy B and C will feel towards A. If they do suffer from envy towards A, this has already been taken into account in the figures and so it remains true that the total happiness in the second distribution is greater than in the first.

The law of diminishing marginal utility underpins the widely held belief that a more equal society is better than one with greater inequality. In the world in which we live, the distribution of income is extraordinarily unequal. Utilitarians should therefore support moves to reduce inequality as long as this does not reduce overall productivity so much that the loss in utility from reduced productivity outweighs the gains from the redistribution of income. Egalitarians may nonetheless feel that, despite this significant agreement on what we ought to do in our present situation, the utilitarian reasons for seeking greater equality fail to give the proper weight to equality as an intrinsic value, independently of its consequences.

Utilitarians differ from egalitarians in that they deny that equality has intrinsic value. Suppose, for example, that the present distribution of happiness is as follows:

(3) A: 10 units; B: 4 units; C: 4 units.

And we have the option of making changes that would result in the following distribution:

(4) A: 3 units; B: 3 units; C: 3 units.

Everyone is better off in (3) than in (4), but (4) is an egalitarian society and (3) is not. Egalitarians are not required to hold that (4) is better than (3); they might say that although equality is an intrinsic value, so is happiness, and in this particular case, the loss of happiness outweighs the increase in equality. They must, however, say that the egalitarian nature of (4) is a reason to prefer it, and that sometimes the value of equality will mean that an egalitarian society is preferable to a less egalitarian one, even if everyone in the egalitarian society is worse off than he or she would be in the less egalitarian society.

One doesn't have to be an egalitarian, however, to object to the fact that utilitarians give no weight to whether a redistribution benefits those who are at the top or the bottom (or to put it more carefully, give no *independent* weight to that fact, since as we have seen, utilitarians do take account of the law of diminishing marginal utility). It is possible to hold that in increasing welfare, we should give priority to those who are worse off, even when that will not bring about the greatest total increase in utility. Prioritarians, as advocates of this view are called, can reject egalitarianism's unpalatable implication that it can be right to make some worse off without making anyone better off, while retaining the intuitively appealing idea that helping those near the bottom is more important than helping those who are better off. Parfit has defended this view.

If egalitarianism and prioritarianism reflect the intrinsic value of equality, or of favouring the worst off, then advocates of these positions face the problem we mentioned in discussing pluralist consequentialism in Chapter 3: how are they to be traded off against other intrinsic values? How *much* priority should we give to greater equality, or to improving the position of the worse off? To make the problem more specific, consider another distribution scenario:

(5) A: 3 units; B: 2 units; C: 1 unit.

Suppose that we can do one, and only one, of the following:

- A: increase A and B's well-being by 5 units each.
- B: increase B's well-being by 2 units.
- C: increase C's well-being by 1 unit and reduce A's well-being by 1 unit.

Which should we do? Utilitarians will say A because that increases well-being by 8 units more than any other option. Prioritarians who put a very high priority on helping the worst off would say C, but if they do not discount benefits to the better off as steeply as that, they might say B or even A. The problem is that there is no principled rationale for choosing any particular discount rate, nor do our intuitions suggest one rate rather than another. Whatever answer is given will therefore seem uncomfortably ad hoc.

There is one argument that may lead utilitarians to move closer to a prioritarian position. If we ask whether we should favour those who are worse off, even if that leads to less well-being overall, prioritarians and egalitarians say yes whereas utilitarians say no. In Chapter 2, we saw that Sidgwick put forward the view that, to the extent that other equally competent judges deny the truth of a proposition that I hold, my own confidence in the truth of that proposition should be reduced, and if I have no more reason to suspect that the other judges are mistaken than I have to suspect that I am mistaken, I should remain neutral between my own view and that of the other judges. Neutrality is all very well on theoretical issues, but what if one has to act, or take a stand on a policy proposal? Given that there are no conclusive arguments that can resolve the disagreement between utilitarians, prioritarians, and egalitarians, and that the philosophers who hold these positions are equally competent, what distributive policies should utilitarians favour? The answer depends on where one stands, relative to those with whom one disagrees. Prioritarians should acknowledge that they may be mistaken and either the egalitarians or the utilitarians may be correct; but as prioritarianism is a middle position between utilitarianism and egalitarianism, and prioritarians cannot say which of these two rivals to their own position is more likely to be correct, they have no reason for doing anything other than follow their own position. Utilitarians, however, are in a different situation, because as compared with utilitarianism, both egalitarians and prioritarians want to give more weight to the interests of the worse off. On the other hand, no one proposes giving more weight to the interests of the better off. Hence utilitarians who acknowledge that they could be wrong on this issue would be justified in giving *some* extra weight to the interests of the worse off, as a kind of moral compromise between different views with strong credentials. This is a way of reducing moral risk: if the utilitarian position is wrong, and either prioritarianism or egalitarianism is right, then at least utilitarians will not be as far off the mark as they would have been if they had simply stuck to the purely utilitarian distribution. How much extra weight utilitarians should give to the worse off is hard to say, in part because prioritarians themselves tend to be vague about how much extra weight they would give, and this vagueness flows through to the compromise position that utilitarians should take.

Chapter 5
Rules

Two forms of utilitarianism

You may know the story of Jean Valjean, the main character of Victor Hugo's novel *Les Misérables*, who stole a loaf of bread to save his starving family and for that crime was sentenced to five years in the galleys. Who would not feel sorry for him? We know there is a moral rule against stealing and we think it good that this rule is generally kept. But it is hard to believe that Valjean did something wrong. A utilitarian can easily explain this judgement. She will gauge the utility or well-being of those involved and conclude that stealing in order to save your family from starvation is not wrong. In contrast, if Valjean had stolen money from a poor person in order to buy himself a beer, that would be wrong.

The form of utilitarianism that judges each individual act in terms of its consequences is known as act-utilitarianism. The most common alternative, rule-utilitarianism, holds that the justification of an act is a two-stage process. Acts are to be judged right or wrong by showing that they are in accord with, or transgress, a justified moral rule; and a moral rule is justified by showing that acceptance of the rule by the overwhelming majority of people will bring about the best outcome.

The main reason for embracing rule-utilitarianism is to avoid some of the troubling implications of utilitarianism that we discussed in Chapter 4. In the sheriff and surgeon cases, the rule-utilitarian might argue that the applicable moral rules are 'Public officials should always obey the law' and 'Doctors should never intentionally harm a patient.' If following these moral rules will have good consequences, then the sheriff and the surgeon should not violate them.

Rule-utilitarianism is very different from act-utilitarianism because sometimes it will prohibit doing what will have the best consequences. J. J. C. Smart asks us to imagine that for a particular moral rule, which he calls R, following the rule will, in 99 per cent of cases, bring about the best possible outcome. Obviously, even for act-utilitarians, R is a useful guide. Often we are too rushed to find out if we are in the 1 per cent of situations in which we could bring about a better outcome by not following R. In these circumstances, knowing that following R almost always brings about the best outcome is sufficient reason to follow R. Suppose, however, that we have plenty of time, there is nothing to bias our judgement, and the evidence is crystal clear that we can achieve a better outcome by not acting in accordance with the rule. Smart asks us to imagine that by breaking the rule we can prevent some avoidable misery, whereas following the rule would do no good at all to anyone. Then, says Smart, to follow the rule would be to turn it into some kind of idol and engage in 'superstitious rule worship'.

Smart has a point. Remember that for the rule-utilitarian the main reason for obeying the rule is that doing so will normally have the best consequences. If because of a general long-term change in relevant circumstances obeying the rule would no longer have the best consequences, the rule-utilitarian would jettison the rule. In this respect the rule-utilitarian's attitude to justifiable rules is not that of a moral absolutist like Anscombe, who, as we saw in Chapter 4, thinks that even to consider a judicial execution of the innocent shows a corrupt mind. Given that rule-utilitarians must be willing to consider such a question, should there be a change in conditions that makes general observance of the rule have bad consequences, it is odd that they insist we continue to obey the rule when we find ourselves in individually unusual circumstances in which doing so will have worse consequences than not obeying it.

At this point the rule-utilitarian may seek to disarm this objection by specifying the rule more precisely. Suppose that the rule is 'Do not steal' and most of the cases in which this rule does not have the best consequences are those in which, like Jean Valjean, by stealing, you achieve some very important good, such as saving someone from starvation. Then we might amend the rule to 'Do not steal unless by stealing you can save someone's life.' That takes care of some of the exceptions, but there are going to be others, where the good achieved is less significant than saving a life, but the person whose property you stole will not be seriously disadvantaged by the loss of the stolen item. We could make an exception for that case, too. But if we continue to refine the rule in this way, eventually we will reach a point where we have covered *all* the circumstances in which an act-utilitarian would steal, and rule-utilitarianism no longer differs, in its practical implications, from act-utilitarianism. If it no longer differs, then the venture into rule-utilitarianism achieves nothing.

It is possible to keep rule-utilitarianism distinct from act-utilitarianism by blocking the extent to which rules can be made more and more detailed and specific. Brad Hooker suggests, in *Ideal Code, Real World*, that the rule to follow is, of all the rules that realistically could be internalized by the community, the one that would have the best consequences if it were internalized. For a rule to be internalized by the community, it has to be sufficiently clear and simple to be applied in everyday life by people who are not going to spend a lot of time working out how a complicated rule might apply to their situation. It must also be suitable for teaching to children. Hence this requirement puts a limit on how many qualifications can be built into a rule, and thus keeps act- and rule-utilitarianism distinct. But that limit raises a further question: what should we do in a situation in which in order to avoid a very bad outcome we would need a more complicated rule that many people would not apply correctly? In 'The ticking bomb' we consider such a situation.

The ticking bomb

A terrorist is captured, together with documents proving his involvement in a plot with others who have hidden a nuclear bomb, primed to detonate in two hours in the midst of Manhattan. The only way to get the terrorist to provide the information needed to stop millions of people being killed is to torture him. Would it be wrong to do so? Philosophers have, for many years, discussed this 'ticking bomb scenario' as a hypothetical example, but the increase in terrorism in the 21st century has brought it closer to reality. Similar situations are now frequently raised in novels, movies, and television dramas. So far, though, there has never been a situation in which the facts are as we have just described, and we are here treating it as a hypothetical example.

'Do not torture' is, for many people, an absolute rule with no exceptions. That is the position taken by the United Nations Convention Against Torture, which states that 'No exceptional circumstances whatsoever, whether a state of war or a threat of war, internal political instability, or any other public emergency, may be invoked as a justification of torture.' There are strong utilitarian reasons in favour of a rule prohibiting torture, and allowing no exceptions. Many documented abuses indicate that without a complete prohibition of torture, interrogators and prison guards will torture their prisoners for all kinds of psychological reasons, perhaps to show their dominance over the prisoners, or perhaps because they are sadists who enjoy making others suffer. Nor, it seems, will a more refined rule work, at least not if we are seeking a rule that can realistically be expected to have the best consequences when accepted by the community. Once we allow exceptions to the prohibition, those who wish to torture will find ways of widening them. The 'no exceptions' language of the UN Convention Against Torture may offer the best prospect of preventing the unjustifiable use of torture.

For utilitarians, especially act-utilitarians, however, there are no acts that cannot be justified by any exceptional circumstances whatsoever. If the standard ticking bomb scenario is not sufficient to convince you of this, we can increase the stakes even further: a group of religious fanatics has taken over a country with a nuclear arsenal large enough to cause the slow and painful extinction from radioactive poisoning of all life on Earth. The group's leader, whose commands are always faithfully obeyed by his followers, has ordered the launch of the entire nuclear arsenal at midnight. This will, he says, bring about Armageddon and the coming of the Messiah. No other country has the military capacity to stop the attack, but a commando force has captured the leader and brought him to a secure hideout. All attempts to reason with him, to persuade him to withdraw his order, have failed, but an expert group has drawn up a psychological profile indicating that he would be unable to resist torture. With only a few hours to go before midnight and no other way of preventing the destruction of life on Earth, utilitarians (and, we believe, anyone who thinks seriously about what is at stake) will conclude that in these circumstances the use of torture is justified. Given that the rule against torture seems like the strongest candidate for an absolutely exceptionless moral rule, it seems that the utilitarians are right to deny that there are any exceptionless moral rules.

Keeping it secret

We seem to face an impossible choice: to support a strict prohibition against torture and take the risk that we will one day find that we have tied our hands against preventing a catastrophe, or to justify torture in some possible, though very unlikely, circumstances, while knowing that this is likely to open the door to the misuse of torture in other circumstances. There is, however, a third possibility: that we publicly support the prohibition while privately advising those who might be in a position of responsibility in a ticking bomb situation to understand that there are some circumstances in which they should violate the prohibition.

This stance is consistent with Sidgwick's careful examination, in *The Methods of Ethics*, of the attitude that utilitarians should have to conventional moral rules that can lead to bad consequences. Sometimes these moral rules need to be reformed or replaced. Yet it may happen that a reformed rule would be too complicated for most people to observe, and this could lead to worse outcomes than retaining the flawed but simpler rule. Utilitarians in that situation should, Sidgwick thought, support the flawed rule in public but not always follow it themselves. When they do break the rule, however, they need to take into account the danger of setting a bad example that will lead others to disregard the rule when it would be better if they followed it. Therefore, Sidgwick wrote, it may be right to do in secret an act that it would be wrong to do or advocate openly and it may also be right to teach or advise one set of people to do something that it would be wrong to teach or advise others to do.

Sidgwick acknowledged that most people find repugnant this idea of an 'esoteric morality'—that is, a morality for 'an enlightened few', different from the morality that most people are taught and expected to follow—but he found the conclusion inescapable. It has been attacked by Bernard Williams, who called it 'Government House utilitarianism'—a phrase that conjures up the idea of a white elite in a grand colonial mansion deciding how best to rule over the 'natives' who they do not regard as capable of participating in these decisions. The colonial associations, however, are irrelevant. Utilitarians take a global perspective and so do not support the imperialist goal of colonizing a developing country to benefit the imperial power. Nevertheless, today Sidgwick's views are likely to be considered politically incorrect. 'Who are you', opponents of esoteric morality will say to utilitarians, 'to assume that you know better than others what ought to be done?'

Utilitarians should, of course, be aware of their own fallibility, and of the tragic consequences that can result from excessive confidence in one's own moral convictions. Yet it is difficult to deny that some people do know better than others what ought to be done—just look at the debate over climate change and what to do about it that has played out in the United States and several other countries over the past two decades. The real problem is to know when one can be sufficiently confident of being right to justify acting on that judgement, even if that means acting contrary to an accepted, and generally desirable, moral rule.

Is utilitarianism self-effacing?

These considerations lead us to two other issues that are distinctive to utilitarian reasoning. Sidgwick wrote: 'It is not necessary that the end which gives the criterion of rightness should always be the end at which we consciously aim.' Philosophers now commonly distinguish between utilitarianism as specifying the standard or criterion for what makes an act right—namely, that it maximizes utility—and utilitarianism as the guide that we use when deciding what is the right thing to do. We may believe that utilitarianism is the right moral theory but at the same time hold that 'Maximize utility' is not the best guide to reaching the right decisions. For example, as act-utilitarians, we can advocate following simple rules in everyday life, knowing that overall this will lead to the best results. If we push things far enough we can even say that as utilitarians we can advocate that people follow Kantian principles like 'never treat another person as a means' or rules against stealing, lying, cheating, and killing the innocent. Philosophers refer to a theory that directs its adherents to follow a different theory as 'self-effacing'. A theory that sometimes, but not always, directs its adherents to follow a different theory is partially self-effacing.

In a spirited response to an objection that is still commonly made today, Bentham shows his awareness of the possibility that utilitarianism is partially self-effacing:

> 'The principle of utility, (I have heard it said) is a dangerous principle: it is dangerous, on certain occasions, to consult it.' This is as much as to say, what? That it is not consonant to utility, to consult utility: in short, that it is *not* consulting it, to consult it.

Nevertheless, the idea that a moral theory could be self-effacing has been severely criticized. What kind of moral theory could be right if, when it comes to putting itself into practice, it rejects itself! Aren't moral theories required to work in practice, and not just in theory?

It's true: moral theories must work in practice. But the fact that utilitarianism is (at least partially) self-effacing does not mean that it fails in practice—it just means that it recommends that we (or some of us, some of the time, if it is only partially self-effacing) adopt non-utilitarian rules or principles and act on them. If that recommendation leads to the utilitarian goal of maximizing utility, then utilitarianism works in practice.

Even if utilitarianism were fully self-effacing, that would be a contingent matter, dependent on circumstances, like our psychological characteristics, or inadequate education, which make it hard for us to think clearly about the consequences of our actions. Should these circumstances change sufficiently, utilitarianism would cease to be self-effacing and would instead tell us to aim directly at maximizing the good. The fact that a theory will in some circumstances be self-effacing does not show that it is not true, for the truth of a normative theory cannot depend on contingent facts about the present state of the world.

The fact that utilitarianism may be partially self-effacing is relevant to a second issue, already mentioned in Chapter 4, concerning when we should praise and blame people. Suppose that we favour preserving a moral rule like 'Do not steal', because it produces better results than if we had to decide every time we have an opportunity to steal whether stealing would maximize the general good. Now, as a result of encouraging people to follow this rule, it happens that someone does not steal even though, had she stolen, she could have saved an innocent person's life. Should we blame this person for letting someone die, and therefore doing something wrong? We saw in Chapter 4 that blaming and praising are acts, and so to decide whether it is right to praise or blame, we must consider the consequences of so doing. In this case, we have to consider the consequences of weakening adherence to the generally useful rule, and so it may be better not to blame the person who failed to save an innocent human life, even though from a utilitarian perspective, considering that act in isolation, it was clearly the wrong thing to do.

There is something paradoxical about all the above problems, and especially about the issue of esoteric morality. Utilitarians are supporting a theory which in some circumstances recommends following other moral theories; and it may be better that the fact that we have utilitarian reasons for recommending these other moral theories should be kept secret. We may give different guidelines to different people on the basis of what we think they will be able to do and how well they will succeed in producing the best consequences, if they aim at them directly. We are ready to bet that you, our readers, are not happy with these conclusions. And it is good that you should not be! We should all be reluctant to embrace esoteric morality. Though utilitarian thinking may, in the world in which we live, lead to esoteric morality, we should follow Sidgwick when he wrote that 'it seems expedient that the doctrine that esoteric morality is expedient should itself be kept esoteric... And thus a Utilitarian may reasonably desire, on Utilitarian principles, that some of his conclusions should be rejected by mankind generally.'

Chapter 6
Utilitarianism in action

Applying utilitarianism today

In 1972 the English philosopher Stuart Hampshire lamented that utilitarianism was no longer the bold, innovative, and even subversive doctrine that it had once been. What Hampshire took to be a long-term decline, however, has proved to be merely a lull in utilitarianism's far-reaching contributions to our changing values and practices. (In what follows we will, for simplicity, be referring mostly to hedonistic utilitarianism, but those who favour other versions of utilitarianism may substitute their own preferred version with little impact on the substance of what we discuss.)

Utilitarianism tells us to reduce suffering and increase happiness. In practice, utilitarians put more emphasis on reducing suffering than on increasing happiness. One reason for this is practical: when people are hungry, cold, and ill, we can alleviate their suffering by providing food, shelter, and health care. When they already have these basic necessities, and are not suffering, it is not so easy to know how to make them happier.

Another, philosophically deeper, reason for focusing on reducing suffering is that there appears to be an asymmetry between suffering and happiness. We are not here suggesting that we should give greater importance to suffering, in itself, than we give to equivalent amounts of happiness. Rather, the asymmetry we are here referring to is an empirical one. The difference can be represented by Figures 10 and 11, in which we assume that the numbers are cardinal, that is, a move from –50 to –49 increases well-being by the same amount as a move from 25 to 26. We also assume that there is a neutral state, in which one is neither happy nor suffering in any way. One way of thinking about such a neutral state is to imagine you have the choice between spending the next hour awake or in a deep dreamless sleep, and everything else is equal—for example, you will not achieve anything, positive or negative, if you are awake, and you will not enjoy waking up feeling refreshed from the sleep.

Figure 10 portrays a symmetrical understanding of suffering and happiness, in which –100 represents the greatest possible suffering, 0 represents a neutral state, and +100 represents the greatest possible happiness. Figure 11 represents a strongly asymmetrical understanding of suffering and happiness in which 0 again represents a neutral state, but the difference between that neutral state and the greatest possible suffering is much greater than the difference between the neutral state and the greatest possible happiness. If our capacity for well-being is accurately represented by Figure 11, then moving someone from the greatest possible suffering to a neutral state far outweighs, in terms of the good it does, moving someone from a neutral state to the greatest possible happiness. This does seem to accord with most people's

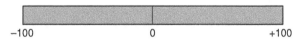

−100 0 +100

10. A symmetrical conception of suffering and happiness.

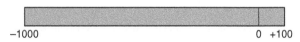

−1000 0 +100

11. An asymmetrical conception of suffering and happiness.

preferences: ask yourself if you would be prepared to undergo, for an hour, the worst suffering you have experienced in order to have an hour of the greatest possible happiness you have experienced. Most people would not. Ask yourself how long the duration of the happiness would have to be to induce you to accept one hour of suffering, and you will have an indication of the extent to which, for you, suffering outweighs happiness.

Social questions are often complex. Attempts to make some people better off are likely to leave others worse off. Given the difficulties of making interpersonal comparisons of utility, which we noticed in Chapter 4, it won't be easy to calculate whether implementing a particular policy will really achieve an increase in net well-being. The best places to apply the theory are therefore those in which it is possible significantly to reduce the suffering of some, with little or no increase in suffering—and ideally, even with little or no reduction in happiness—to others. Such situations are, for utilitarians, the low-hanging fruit. One might wonder why such fruit has not been picked long ago—that is, why policies have not already been changed to prevent such easily avoidable suffering. Sometimes the answer is that eliminating the suffering requires abandoning a key element of traditional morality; in other situations the suffering may be experienced by a group whose interests are disregarded. We will start with a case in the first of these categories.

End of life decisions

In 2009 Gloria Taylor, a Canadian, was told she had amyotrophic lateral sclerosis (or ALS), which causes progressive muscle weakness. ALS patients gradually lose the use of their hands and feet, and then become unable to walk, chew, swallow, and speak. When they lose the ability to breathe, they die. Rather than accept this distressing and inevitable progression towards death, Taylor wanted her doctor to assist her to die at a time of her own choosing (see Figure 12).

12. Gloria Taylor, whose court action brought all Canadians the right
to physician assistance in dying.

If Taylor had needed some kind of life support, like a respirator,
a doctor would have been able to turn it off, even if it were
certain that turning it off would bring about Taylor's death. Yet in
Canada, as in many other countries, because Taylor's life was not
dependent on medical technology, it was illegal for a doctor to act
on her request. Taylor went to court to challenge this law.

The legal distinction between what is sometimes called 'passive
euthanasia'—that is, bringing about a patient's death by
withholding or withdrawing treatment—and 'active euthanasia' or
'physician-assisted dying' reflects a traditional ethical view, based
on the idea that it is always wrong to take an innocent person's
life. Advocates of rule-based ethics frequently find themselves
drawing fine lines that demarcate where a rule applies and where
it does not, and so decisions of great consequence can hinge on
something that any thinking person can see is ethically irrelevant,
such as whether a patient's death is brought about by turning
off a switch on a machine, or by writing the patient a prescription

for a drug with which she can end her life. It is a strength of utilitarianism that it focuses on aspects of decisions that are clearly relevant, like pain and pleasure, or what a person most wants, and not on tenuous distinctions between what does, and what does not, amount to a killing.

Admittedly, one does not have to be a utilitarian to oppose laws that make it a crime for a doctor to assist a patient like Taylor to die. One might question such laws on the basis of a 'right to die' which can be seen as part of a broader right to autonomy in matters that primarily concern oneself. But how do we establish that there are such rights, and that the right to die extends to the right to receive assistance in dying? Claims based on rights amount to little more than asserting an intuition that others will deny. In contrast, once we start to consider the consequences of holding that it is always wrong to kill an innocent person, we find that the usual reasons against killing do not apply to terminally ill patients who are suffering and request assistance in dying. Normally, of course, killing an innocent person will have very bad consequences. If we assume that a human life generally has more happiness than suffering, then the direct consequence of killing someone is to deprive the victim of all the happiness he or she would otherwise have enjoyed. The indirect consequences are in some cases even worse: grief and a sense of loss, often long-lasting, for those who loved the person killed, and heightened insecurity for everyone who learns about the killing. Violent crimes like killing threaten our sense that we are in control of our lives, and our confidence in our ability to determine our own future, and lead us to change our behaviour in order to reduce the risk of being killed, forgoing pleasures like walking home late at night.

Now consider Gloria Taylor's situation. The relentless progress of ALS was bound to mean that at some point her life would contain much more suffering than happiness, and this state would continue until her death. So a doctor who at that point acted on her request and helped her to die would be preventing further suffering, rather than depriving her of happiness. Moreover, since Taylor would have intentionally brought about her own death, and the doctor would be acting on her request, her death would not cause anxiety or insecurity to anyone else; in fact, it would reduce the anxiety many terminally ill patients feel about the way in which they will die. Those who love her would not wish her to suffer beyond the point at which she considered her life worth living, and the grief they would experience at her death would not be greater because the death came a few weeks earlier than it would have come if the disease had been allowed to run its natural course.

The utilitarian arguments for permitting doctors to assist patients to end their lives are much clearer and more decisive than rights-based arguments. Reaching this conclusion about individual cases is not, however, the end of the discussion about what the law should be. Utilitarians still need to ask if changing the law would have other bad consequences. That question was closely examined by Justice Lynn Smith in the case that Taylor brought. She heard evidence from international experts in medicine, law, psychology, and bioethics, and examined the experience of jurisdictions such as the Netherlands and Oregon, where physicians had for more than a decade been able to help patients to die. She paid particular attention to whether, in those jurisdictions, elderly or ill people are pressured to accept assistance in dying. She concluded that this is not the case, and that suitably designed laws can permit some to die in the way they wish, while protecting vulnerable people who wish to continue to live. Justice Smith's decision was upheld by the Supreme Court of Canada, and as a result, terminally ill Canadians now have a legal right to medical assistance in dying.

Ethics and animals

The unnecessary suffering of terminally ill patients who want to die continues, in many countries, because when it comes to killing, few people are willing to challenge traditional morality and the aura of sanctity that it spreads over human life, irrespective of its quality or the wishes of the person living it. Sadly, these same moral views do not restrict the killing of non-human animals at all. Indeed, not only is killing permitted for sport, for fur, and because we enjoy the taste of an animal's flesh, but the enormous amount of unnecessary suffering that we inflict on animals is proof that we give little or no weight to any interests of non-human animals, including their interest in not suffering.

This is not how utilitarians regard animals. Although utilitarian views about the painless killing of animals vary, all the leading utilitarians are clear that suffering is no less bad when it is the suffering of an animal than when it is the suffering of a human. At the outset of this book we quoted Jeremy Bentham looking forward to the time 'when humanity will extend its mantle over everything which breathes'. In another passage, in a footnote to his *Introduction to the Principles of Morals and Legislation*, he pointed out that the differences between humans and animals are insufficient reasons for abandoning them to 'the caprice of a tormentor'. The question is not, he said, 'Can they *reason*? nor, Can they *talk*? but, Can they *suffer*?'

The utilitarian insistence on the significance of animal suffering follows directly from the utilitarian principle that we should seek the largest possible surplus of pleasure over pain, coupled with the obvious fact that animals are capable of experiencing pleasure and pain. This common-sense observation is now supported by a considerable body of scientific evidence that was not available to 19th-century utilitarians. We know that vertebrate animals respond to pain and pleasure much as we do, both in the function of the central nervous system, and behaviourally, as well as in the specific regions of the brain that are active when we experience pain or pleasure. Some invertebrates may also be capable of pleasure and pain—certainly octopuses appear to be capable of thinking their way to solutions to novel problems. Consistently with this principle, Mill and Sidgwick agreed with Bentham that the suffering of animals matters. Mill went so far as to say that he was prepared to stake the entire question of the validity of the principle of utilitarianism on the inclusion of animals in morality. Here he is, writing in response to a critic who attacked utilitarianism for implying that it could be right to sacrifice the happiness of humans in order to improve the lives of animals:

> Granted that any practice causes more pain to animals than it gives pleasure to man; is that practice moral or immoral? And if, exactly in proportion as human beings raise their heads out of the slough of selfishness, they do not with one voice answer 'immoral,' let the morality of the principle of utility be for ever condemned.

Mill leaves us in no doubt that he rejects any discounting of the interests of animals, as compared with humans, assuming instead that the pains of animals count *equally* with the pleasures of humans. He is, in essence, arguing for equal consideration of similar interests, irrespective of the species of the being whose interests are being considered. He is thus objecting to 'speciesism' before the term had been invented.

When Bentham wrote his comments on extending protection to all sentient beings there were no laws, in England or anywhere else in the world, against cruelty to animals. Even today, more than two centuries later, the laws protecting animals from cruelty fall well short of what Bentham and Mill advocated. Factory farming is the most obvious of many contemporary practices regarding animals that utilitarianism clearly shows to be indefensible. An estimated 65 billion vertebrate land animals are killed for food every year, and most of them are raised in appallingly crowded and confined conditions on factory farms (see Figure 13). Nor is this practice necessary to provide us with food. On the contrary, when we take animals off the fields and lock them in cages, stalls, sheds, or feedlots, we have to grow grains and

13. Factory farmed pigs spend all their lives confined in small spaces.

soybeans to feed to them. The animals use most of the food value of these crops simply in order to keep warm and move around; we get back only a small fraction of the food value we put into them. Aside from the immense waste of food this involves and the deleterious effect that eating so much meat has on our health, factory farming causes a vast amount of suffering to animals and adds significantly to our greenhouse gas emissions. If we consider that all this exists only to satisfy human desires to eat something with a particular taste or texture, it is obvious that the intensive raising of animals for food is contrary to the utilitarian view that the pain and suffering of animals should count equally with similar amounts of human pain and suffering. Once again, there are other ethical views that reach the same conclusion, but utilitarians have been pioneers in this area, and their arguments are, in our view, the clearest and strongest.

The use of animals for research is a more difficult question, because the possible benefits from this use of animals are much greater than those from the use of animals for food, at least for people who are able to nourish themselves adequately in other ways. Here a utilitarian may differ from a proponent of animal rights, because on some views of rights, they are absolute, and therefore not to be outweighed by any good consequences that would come from violating them. Absolutist rights advocates are thus spared the necessity of investigating the possible costs of ending experimentation on animals; utilitarians are not.

Millions of harmful experiments on animals serve no urgent purpose. They may, for example, be carried out to test the safety of new cosmetics or household products, when the products are being developed to profit the manufacturer, rather than to meet some important need of consumers. Yet not all experiments on animals can be so easily dismissed. Some do advance medical knowledge. We cannot know in advance which ones these will be, but when there is:

- a reasonable chance of discovering how to prevent or cure a disease that brings suffering and/or death to large numbers of people or animals; and
- no other way to achieve this goal without the use of some animals (but many fewer than the number of people or animals that the discovery would help); and
- all possible steps are taken to reduce any pain and suffering the animals may experience; and
- there is no other way of using the money, time, and skill that goes into the research that would produce more good overall;

then

- the use of animals for research will be justifiable.

This discussion of how animals should be treated has been based entirely on the principle of equal consideration of their interests in not suffering, and not on any claims about the wrongness of killing animals. Bentham thought that killing animals for food is not wrong:

> …there is very good reason why we should be suffered to eat such of them as we like to eat: we are the better for it, and they are never the worse. They have none of those long-protracted anticipations of future misery which we have.

In pointing out that animals do not anticipate their death, in the way that normal humans do, Bentham was drawing attention to a relevant difference; but why does he suggest that animals are 'never the worse' for being killed? If they would otherwise have had a surplus of pleasure over pain, then killing them makes them worse off in a very straightforward way that a utilitarian should condemn. Perhaps, though, Bentham was making a different and more subtle point that has subsequently been made by many defenders of meat-eating: if we did not eat them, the pigs, cows, and chickens killed would never have existed. There were no factory farms in Bentham's time, so the lives of most animals raised for food would have been better than today, and arguably positive, even in the absence of humane slaughter laws. Perhaps therefore when Bentham wrote that 'they are never the worse' he meant that animals in general are not worse off because of the practice of raising and killing them for food. If so, he was contributing to a debate that continues today and that raises issues that are also relevant to questions about human population that we will touch upon later in this chapter.

Effective altruism

Utilitarians tend to be reformers, but their reforms can be either of the political right or left, depending on whether they think that an unfettered free market is the best way of enabling everyone to prosper, or believe that the state needs to ensure that everyone's basic needs are met. Bentham, who wrote extensively on the causes of poverty and on the reform of the Poor Laws, was among the latter. Unusually for his time, he did not restrict assistance to the 'deserving' poor. Even when someone's poverty is the result of acting irresponsibly, the pain of death, Bentham pointed out, clearly outweighs the pain to the taxpayer of funding relief to keep the person from starving.

In the more progressive affluent countries today, governments ensure that all their citizens, and usually all those living within their borders, have the means to obtain not only enough to eat, but also at least basic health care. The sufferings caused by lack of food or basic health care are not, however, any less for people living beyond the borders of affluent countries than they are for those within. In Bentham's time communications and transport were too slow to enable people to give effective aid to those who were starving in a distant country. Now those obstacles have been overcome, and the problem of extreme poverty requires a global approach. Over the past fifty years, with support from utilitarians as well as the followers of some major religions, there has been significant progress in reducing extreme poverty. In 2015, probably for the first time in the existence of our species, the proportion of people living in extreme poverty fell below 10 per cent, while the number of children dying before their fifth birthday fell from 20 million in 1960 to fewer than 6 million in 2015, despite the world's population having more than doubled during that period.

These figures are encouraging. Yet in a world in which more than a billion people are living in affluence and spending vast sums on luxury consumer goods, the fact that 700 million people are living in extreme poverty and nearly 6 million children die each year from avoidable, poverty-related causes indicates that extreme poverty is still causing a vast amount of human suffering that could be prevented.

Effective altruism is a response to this situation. It began in 2009 when Toby Ord founded Giving What We Can, an organization that informs people how much good they can do by donating to the most highly effective organizations. Peter Singer's widely reprinted essay 'Famine, Affluence and Morality' played a role, as did Nick Bostrom's writings emphasizing the importance of reducing the risk of human extinction. Will MacAskill worked with Ord to set up Giving What We Can, soon followed by other organizations such as GiveWell, Less Wrong, and The Life You Can Save, all of which combined to develop effective altruism into a worldwide movement. Ord and MacAskill are Oxford philosophers who describe themselves as having more credence in utilitarianism than in any other positive moral view (the cautious phrasing allows for uncertainty about what is the right moral view). Because effective altruism encourages us to help others as effectively as we can, it is clear that utilitarians ought to be effective altruists, and in a 2015 survey of nearly 3,000 effective altruists, 56 per cent described themselves as utilitarians. Of course, that still leaves a substantial proportion of effective altruists holding non-utilitarian moral views. That is not surprising, because there are many different moral views that imply that we ought to help others as effectively as possible, as long as we are not violating some moral rules or acting contrary to some virtues. Nevertheless, effective altruism is perhaps the clearest example of how utilitarianism today is making a difference to how people act and the amount of good they do.

Effective altruism takes an impartial perspective on whom we should help. The goal is to do the most good we can with whatever resources we are prepared to apply to that objective, and if we can do more good by helping people in a developing country than in our own community, that is what we should do. The same impartial perspective applies to the choice between present and future: effective altruists discount the future only to the extent that we are less certain about the impact of what we do when that impact will not be felt until some future period.

Effective altruists emphasize the importance of using evidence to decide what will do the most good, and one of the movement's most important contributions has been to assess the available evidence for the causes and organizations that appear to be highly effective in helping others. From this assessment has come the remarkable finding that some charities are hundreds of times more effective than others. Toby Ord compared the effectiveness of donating to an organization that trains guide dogs to help blind people with donating to an organization that prevents people in developing countries from becoming, or remaining, blind. He found that it costs about $US40,000 to train one guide dog, but as little as $25 to prevent someone going blind because of trachoma, the leading cause of blindness in developing countries. Preventing someone from going blind seems to be better, in most cases, than giving a blind person a guide dog, so on Ord's figures, donating to an organization combating trachoma is *at least* 1,600 times more effective than donating to an organization training guide dogs.

Effective altruists are more concerned about outcomes than about moral merit, and hence are not troubled about whether someone is acting in a purely altruistic way, rather than because he or she is interested in gaining a good reputation, or living a more fulfilling life. For that reason they point to research showing that people who are generous are more satisfied with their lives than those who do less to help others.

Effective altruists regard reducing global poverty as one possible way of doing the most good, but some effective altruists believe that we can do more good by reducing animal suffering, while others argue that because we tend to disregard small risks of major catastrophes, we are not giving sufficient thought to reducing the danger of our own extinction. Possible causes of our extinction include nuclear war, a large asteroid colliding with our planet, a pandemic, whether natural or as a result of bioterrorism, and superintelligent computers that turn on their creators.

It is difficult to say how important it is to reduce these risks of extinction, and not only because the risks themselves, and our ability to reduce them, are difficult to quantify. A deeper issue is whether, in making such calculations, we should take into account only the existing lives that will be lost if an extinction event occurs—that is, the more than 7 billion people who would be killed if it were to happen today—or if we should also include the untold trillions (or perhaps many orders of magnitude more than that) of lives prevented from ever existing. Against including merely possible beings, it can be said that it makes no sense to talk about harming a non-existent being, so no one is made worse off by the fact that these possible beings will never exist. On the other hand if we regard human life as positive—and most of us surely do—then there seems to be some loss of value if there are going to be no future human beings. The loss is, admittedly, not to any actual person, but we might say that the universe as a whole would have less value if there were no intelligent beings living rich and fulfilling lives in our particular part of it, or possibly, anywhere in it at all. Even if we do not treat the prevention of the life of a possible being as on a par with the loss of life of an actual being, if we give any weight at all to the existence of merely possible beings, then the vast numbers of such lives that are likely to be prevented from existing by our extinction dramatically increases the importance of preventing such an event. For if we can avoid extinction in the next century or two, we may be able to colonize other planets, thus protecting our species against disasters that happen on any one planet, and ensuring our survival for millions or even billions of years.

In response to this line of thought, there is now a community of effective altruists who are, on utilitarian grounds, encouraging and carrying out research into ways of minimizing various specific risks of human extinction.

Population puzzles

The question that emerged from our discussion of the risk of human extinction is related to an issue in population ethics that was first raised by Sidgwick. He noticed that in some circumstances it will be possible to increase the total amount of happiness by bringing more people into existence, even though this means that the average level of happiness falls (because of greater crowding or reduced resources per person). So the question arises whether utilitarians should aim at the highest average level of happiness, or the greatest total. Sidgwick thought that they should aim at the greatest total.

Sidgwick was right to reject the average view. Imagine that the known world consists of Paradise, a large continent that is home to one billion of the happiest people you can possibly imagine, living rich and enjoyable lives free of war, violence, and disease. The Paradise Office of Statistics issues an annual World Happiness Report that reports on the average happiness level of all the people in the world that it knows about. On a scale that goes from 0 to 100, the level in Paradise is mostly around 99. Then explorers sail across the ocean and discover Halcyon, a new continent in which there are another billion people, also living rich and enjoyable lives free of war, violence, and disease. Because the weather is not quite so pleasant in Halcyon as it is in Paradise, however, their level of happiness is, on the scale used by the Paradise statisticians, around 90.

When the statisticians on Paradise compile their next World Happiness Report, they note that the inhabitants of Paradise are so delighted that another inhabited continent has been discovered that their own average happiness has risen to 100. Nevertheless, because the newly discovered inhabitants of Halcyon are included for the first time, the world average happiness level has fallen to 95. For proponents of the average view, this must be a bad thing. But it is hardly plausible to regard the existence of a billion people, all leading rich and enjoyable lives, with just a few rainy days to dampen their enjoyment, as a bad thing. For whom is it bad? Not for the inhabitants of Paradise, whose average level of happiness has gone up because of the discovery of a new continent and a new culture. Surely not, however, for the inhabitants of Halcyon, who are very satisfied with their lives and not in the least jealous of their newfound friends on slightly sunnier Paradise. As this example shows, the average view implies that the world can get worse, though no one in it has been harmed in the slightest degree, and the difference between the happiness levels of different populations is not the result of inegalitarian policies or individual actions. That seems wrong.

Should we then accept the total view? Before we do, we must take account of its own uncongenial implications. It implies that for any world full of people living rich, fulfilling, and extremely happy lives, there would be a *better* world in which everyone's life is just barely positive—let's say that they have slightly more pleasure than pain. This world of people whose lives are just barely positive will, according to the total view, be *better* than the world full of extremely happy people, as long as the population is large enough for the sum of all the barely positive lives to add up to a greater total quantity of happiness. It may, of course, have to be a world with a huge population, far beyond what our planet can at present cope with, but this thought experiment is not constrained by the limits of Earth. The question is, would you really think the world with the greater total quantity of happiness is the better world?

If neither the average nor the total view is satisfactory, what theory does better? Since Derek Parfit first discussed these questions in the 1970s, philosophers have been looking for what he called 'Theory X'—a theory that is inherently plausible and can reconcile the strong intuitions we have about these cases. No such theory has been found, and it may be that no such theory is possible. This is not, however, a problem that is specific to utilitarianism. Any ethical theory should be able to say in what circumstances it would be desirable for governments to seek to encourage couples to have larger families, and in what circumstances it is desirable for couples to bring children into the world rather than to remain childless or adopt existing children in need of a home.

Many people will find the answer obvious, given concerns about whether the Earth can sustain the population of around 10 billion people that is predicted to be reached by 2050. Nevertheless the question of whether it is good, other things being equal, to bring into the world children who can be expected to live happy lives remains, on some optimistic views of our planet's future, a real one.

Gross national happiness

Although Paradise and Halcyon are, unfortunately, imaginary places, there really is a World Happiness Report. The first report was published in 2012 by an independent group of experts for a United Nations High Level Meeting on Happiness and Well-Being. That meeting followed a UN General Assembly resolution that invited member countries to recognize happiness as a 'fundamental human goal', to measure the happiness of their people, and to use this measure in forming their public policies. Such a proposal is obviously very much in accord with utilitarian thinking.

The UN resolution was moved by the Prime Minister of Bhutan, a small Himalayan kingdom that has been the pioneer in promoting 'gross national happiness'. In Bhutan a Gross National Happiness Commission, chaired by the Prime Minister, assesses all new policy proposals put forward by government ministries. Policies found to be contrary to the goal of promoting gross national happiness are sent back to the ministry for reconsideration. If they do not ultimately receive the Commission's approval, they will not go ahead. In keeping with the goal of promoting national happiness, Bhutan prohibits the sale of cigarettes and other forms of tobacco.

We may agree that our goal ought to be promoting happiness, rather than income or gross domestic product, but in view of the difficulties of measuring happiness discussed in Chapter 4, is it feasible to take happiness as an indicator of the success of government policies? Two main approaches to measuring happiness are currently being used by social scientists and polling organizations. One tries to add up the number of positive moments that people have, and then to subtract the negative ones. If the result is substantially positive, we regard the person's life as happy; if negative, as unhappy. So, to measure happiness defined in that way, we have to sample moments of people's existence randomly and try to find out whether they are experiencing positive or negative mental states. The second approach asks people: 'How satisfied are you with the way your life has gone so far?' If they say they are satisfied, or very satisfied, they are happy, rather than unhappy. On surveys that use the first approach, countries like Nigeria, Mexico, Brazil, and Puerto Rico do well, which suggests that the answer may have more to do with the national culture than with objective indicators like health, education, and standard of living. When the second approach is taken, it tends to be the richer countries like Denmark and Switzerland that come out on top. But it is not clear whether people's answers to survey questions in different languages and in different cultures really mean the same thing.

Since the UN resolution on recognizing happiness as a fundamental human goal, several international and national organizations have investigated how best to measure happiness. The Organization for Economic Cooperation and Development launched a Better Life Initiative which led, in 2013, to a set of guidelines aimed at assisting governments to measure the well-being of their citizens. The guidelines reflect the increasing body of evidence showing that measures of subjective well-being are reliable and can provide a basis for policy-making. The United Nations Development Programme has also added national average life evaluations to the development statistics it produces. With more scientists working on measuring happiness and understanding what increases it, the idea of happiness as a fundamental goal of public policy is gaining support. Bentham would have been pleased.

Further reading and notes on sources

General

Recent introductory works on utilitarianism include: Krister Bykvist, *Utilitarianism: A Guide for the Perplexed*, Bloomsbury Academic, London, 2010 and Tim Mulgan, *Understanding Utilitarianism*, Routledge, London, 2014. Those who want to go more deeply into the topic may wish to read Katarzyna de Lazari-Radek and Peter Singer, *The Point of View of the Universe*, Oxford University Press, Oxford, 2014, or Torbjörn Tännsjö, *Hedonistic Utilitarianism*, Edinburgh University Press, Edinburgh, 1998. For specific topics discussed in this book, we also recommend looking up the topic in the free online *Stanford Encyclopedia of Philosophy*: <https://plato.stanford.edu>.

Preface

The initial quotations are from the following sources:

On animals: Jeremy Bentham, *Principles of Penal Law*, Part III, ch. 16, in *The Works of Jeremy Bentham*, ed. J. Bowring, William Tait, Edinburgh, 1838, p. 562.

On homosexuality: Jeremy Bentham, from a manuscript in the University College, London, Bentham manuscripts, folder lxxiv(a), sheet 6, quoted by Faramerz Dabhoiwala, *The Origins of Sex*, Allen Lane, London, 2012, p. 135.

On women: John Stuart Mill, *The Subjection of Women*, Longmans Green, London, 1869. The first passage is from ch. 1, and the second from ch. 3.

Karl Marx's comment on Bentham is from his *Capital*, vol. 1, ch. XXIV, sect. 5, Penguin, London, 1992 (first published 1867). Friedrich Nietzsche's reference to utilitarianism is in *Beyond Good and Evil*, sect. 260, Penguin, London, 1973 (first published 1886), trans. R. J. Hollingdale. Bernard Williams's attack on utilitarianism was published in J. J. C. Smart and Bernard Williams, *Utilitarianism: For or Against*, Cambridge University Press, Cambridge, 1973, where the comment quoted is on p. 150. Philippa Foot's quote is from her 'Utilitarianism and the Virtues', *Mind*, 94 (1985), p. 196.

Chapter 1: Origins

A good introductory book on the history of utilitarianism is Frederick Rosen, *Classical Utilitarianism from Hume to Mill*, Routledge, London, 2003. Bart Schultz, *The Happiness Philosophers*, Princeton University Press, Princeton, 2017, focuses on the lives and works of William Godwin, Jeremy Bentham, John Stuart and Harriet Taylor Mill, and Henry Sidgwick.

Ancient precursors

On Mozi, see *The Stanford Encyclopedia of Philosophy* on Mohism by Chris Fraser, available at <https://plato.stanford.edu/entries/mohism>. Another useful source is Chad Hansen, 'Mozi: Language Utilitarianism: The Structure of Ethics in Classical China', *The Journal of Chinese Philosophy* 16 (1989), pp. 355–80. Further information is available on the Hong Kong University site, <http://www.philosophy.hku.hk/ch/moencyred.html>.

On Buddhist ethics with some indications of utilitarian tendencies, see Chao-hwei Shih, *Buddhist Normative Ethics*, Dharma-Dhatu Publications, Taoyuan, Taiwan, 2014.

For Epicurus, see *The Stanford Encyclopedia of Philosophy* article by David Konstan: <https://plato.stanford.edu/entries/epicurus/>.

The early utilitarians

The sources of the quotations from the early utilitarians are as follows:

Richard Cumberland, *De legibus naturae*, ch. 5, sect. IX, first published 1672; we have quoted the first English translation, by John Maxwell, first published in 1727 and repr. by Liberty Fund, Indianapolis, 2005. (This and the following two works, along with many other classic texts, are available online from the Liberty Fund.)

Anthony Ashley Cooper, Earl of Shaftesbury, *Characteristicks of Men, Manners, Opinions, Times*, Liberty Fund, Indianapolis, 2001, vol. 1, p. 37.

Frances Hutcheson, *An Inquiry into the Original of our Ideas of Beauty and Virtue*, Liberty Fund, Indianapolis, 2004 (first published 1726), treatise ii, section iii, paragraph VIII.

Bentham's comment on the scales falling from his eyes, and on his dedicating his life to promoting the greatest happiness, are from a footnote to ch. 1 of his *A Fragment on Government*, ed. J. H. Burns and H. L. A. Hart, Cambridge University Press, Cambridge, 1988 (first published anonymously in 1776).

Joachim Hruschka argues that German thinkers were among the first to anticipate utilitarian ideas, in 'The Greatest Happiness Principle and Other Early German Anticipations of Utilitarian Theory', *Utilitas*, 3 (1991), pp. 165–77.

The founder: Bentham

Bentham's only published work that is explicitly on utilitarian theory is *Introduction to the Principles of Morals and Legislation*, written in 1780 and first published, with some additional material, in 1789. It is available in several print editions, as well as online.

Those interested in transcribing Bentham's unpublished manuscripts should go to: <https://www.ucl.ac.uk/Bentham-Project/transcribe_bentham>.

Samuel Johnson's views on punishing 'irregular intercourse' are cited from Faramerz Dabhoiwala, 'Lust and Liberty', *Past and Present*, 207 (2010), p. 150; the same article contains, on pp. 168–74, a useful summary of Bentham's writing on sexual morality. For a selection of these writings, see Jeremy Bentham, *Of Sexual Irregularities, and Other Writings on Sexual Morality*, ed. Philip Schofield, Catherine Pease-Watkin, and Michael Quinn, Clarendon Press, Oxford, 2014. Specific passages described in the text are from pp. 112 and 148 of this volume.

The advocate: John Stuart Mill

Mill's *Utilitarianism* was first published as a series of three articles in 1861 and then as a book two years later. It is available in several print editions and online. For more discussion of Mill's utilitarianism, see Roger Crisp, *On Utilitarianism*, Routledge, London, 1997 and

The Blackwell Guide to Mill's Utilitarianism, ed. Henry West, Wiley-Blackwell, London, 2006.

Mill's description of his feelings on reading Bentham is to be found in his *Autobiography*, Penguin, London, 1990 (first published 1873), ch. 3.

The academic philosopher: Henry Sidgwick

Sidgwick's most important work is *The Methods of Ethics*. The first edition was published in 1874, but Sidgwick revised it throughout his life. The most widely used edition is the 7th, published after the author's death, in 1907, and available both in print editions and online.

Smart expressed his high opinion of Sidgwick's work in his 'Extreme and Restricted Utilitarianism', *Philosophical Quarterly*, 25 (1956), pp. 344–54. Parfit's is from *On What Matters*, vol. 1, Oxford University Press, Oxford, 2011, p. xxxiii. The best account of Sidgwick's life is Bart Schultz, *Henry Sidgwick: Eye of the Universe*, Cambridge University Press, Cambridge, 2004, and our statement about Sidgwick's romantic inclinations is based on the evidence Schultz lays out on pp. 414–15. Jerome Schneewind, *Sidgwick's Ethics and Victorian Moral Philosophy*, Clarendon Press, Oxford, 1977, is a classic study of *The Methods of Ethics*, while more recent works include David Phillips, *Sidgwickian Ethics*, Oxford University Press, Oxford, 2011, Katarzyna de Lazari-Radek and Peter Singer, *The Point of View of the Universe*, Oxford University Press, Oxford, 2014, and Roger Crisp, *The Cosmos of Duty*, Oxford University Press, Oxford, 2015.

Chapter 2: Justification

Bentham on justifying the utilitarian principle

Descartes advocated his foundationalist method in his *Discourse on Method* (1637) and used it in his *Meditations on First Philosophy* (1641) in which he argued that 'I think, therefore I am' provides an indubitable foundation for knowledge. Rawls put forward the idea of reflective equilibrium in *A Theory of Justice*, Belknap Press of Harvard University Press, Cambridge, Mass., 1971, revised edition 1999.

The flow chart is based on *An Introduction to the Principles of Morals and Legislation*, ch. 1, para. XIV.

Mill's proof

Mill's *Utilitarianism* was ranked as the second most widely used text
in philosophy courses by The Open Syllabus Project (<http://www.
opensyllabusproject.org?>, last viewed 11 January 2017). His
'proof' of the principle of utility is the subject of ch. 4 of his
Utilitarianism.

Sidgwick's proof

Sidgwick's critical examination of the morality of common sense
occupies Book III of *The Methods of Ethics*. Ch. 11 of that Book is a
summary of his arguments, and it is in sect. 2 of that chapter that
Sidgwick sets out the four conditions that a proposition must meet
to be self-evident. In ch. 13 of Book III he argues for the axioms of
justice, prudence, and benevolence.

Harsanyi's argument from rational choice under conditions of ignorance

Harsanyi used the device of choice from a position of ignorance in
'Cardinal Welfare, Individualistic Ethics, and Interpersonal
Comparisons of Utility', *Journal of Political Economy*, 63/4 (Aug.
1955), pp. 309–32, especially at p. 316; for an earlier, briefer
statement, see John Harsanyi, 'Cardinal Utility in Welfare
Economics and in the Theory of Risk-Taking', *Journal of Political
Economy*, 61/5 (Oct. 1953), pp. 434–5. Rawls argues that the veil of
ignorance would lead the parties to choose the two principles of
justice in sect. 26 of *A Theory of Justice*; for a demonstration of the
unconvincing nature of the arguments of this section of the book,
see Brian Barry, *The Liberal Theory of Justice*, Clarendon Press,
Oxford, 1973, especially ch. 9. Harsanyi formalized his argument
for utilitarianism in 'Bayesian Decision Theory and Utilitarian
Ethics', *The American Economic Review*, 68 (1978), pp. 223–8.
For discussion about his proof, see Hilary Greaves, 'A
Reconsideration of the Harsanyi–Sen–Weymark Debate on
Utilitarianism', *Utilitas* (2016), pp. 1–39. doi: 10.1017/
S0953820816000169 (print version forthcoming).

Smart's appeal to attitudes and feelings

Smart's *An Outline of a System of Utilitarian Ethics* was first
published by Melbourne University Press in 1961; a revised version
later appeared as part of J. J. C. Smart and Bernard Williams,
Utilitarianism For & Against, Cambridge University Press,

Cambridge, 1973. The quotations from Smart are from this later version, pp. 7–8.

Hare's universal prescriptivism

Hare discusses universalizability in his books *Freedom and Reason*, Oxford University Press, Oxford, 1963, and in *Moral Thinking*, Oxford University Press, Oxford, 1981. For a shorter statement of his position, see R. M. Hare, 'Universal Prescriptivism', in Peter Singer, ed., *A Companion to Ethics*, Blackwell, Oxford, 1991, where the account of universalizability is on p. 456. George Bernard Shaw's response to the Golden Rule is from 'Maxims for Revolutionists', an appendix to his play *Man and Superman*, Penguin, London, 2001 (first published 1905). Hare first argued that universalizability leads to utilitarianism in 'Ethical Theory and Utilitarianism', in H. D. Lewis, ed., *Contemporary British Philosophy 4*, Allen and Unwin, London, 1976; repr. in R. M. Hare, *Essays in Ethical Theory*, Clarendon Press, Oxford, 1989. He developed the argument more fully in *Moral Thinking*, Oxford University Press, Oxford, 1981. *Moral Thinking* also includes Hare's discussion of amoralism—see especially p. 186.

For a compendium of 'Golden Rules' in many different texts and cultures, see Howard Terry, *Golden Rules and Silver Rules of Humanity*, Infinity Publishing, West Conshoschoken, Pa., 2011.

Greene: arguing for utilitarianism by debunking opposing principles

On the errors made by some sociobiologists who have sought to deduce values from facts about evolution, see Peter Singer, *The Expanding Circle*, 2nd edn, Princeton University Press, Princeton, 2011.

Greene's argument for utilitarianism is most explicitly presented in 'Beyond Point-and-Shoot Morality: Why Cognitive (Neuro)Science Matters for Ethics', *Ethics*, 124 (July 2014), pp. 695–726. His earlier book, *Moral Tribes: Emotion, Reason, and the Gap Between Us and Them*, Penguin, New York, 2013, gave a fuller statement of the research on which his argument is based.

The original statement of the trolley problem is in Philippa Foot, 'The Problem of Abortion and the Doctrine of Double Effect', *Oxford Review*, 5 (1967), pp. 5–15. It was then developed by Judith Jarvis Thomson, 'The Trolley Problem', *Yale Law Journal*, 94 (1985), pp. 1395–415. Book-length discussions are David Edmonds, *Would You Kill the Fat Man?*, Princeton University Press, Princeton, 2013, and Thomas Cathcart, *The Trolley Problem*, Workman, New York, 2013. The statement that most people respond to *Loop* in the same way as *Switch* is supported by Experiment 2 described in Michael Waldman and Jörn Dieterich, 'Throwing a Bomb on a Person Versus Throwing a Person on a Bomb: Intervention Myopia in Moral Decisions', *Psychological Science*, 18 (2007), pp. 247–53.

Dual process theory was first suggested by Seymour Epstein, 'Integration of the Cognitive and the Psychodynamic Unconscious', *American Psychologist*, 49 (1994), pp. 709–24, and has been developed by many other scientists over the past two decades. An accessible statement is Daniel Kahneman, *Thinking Fast and Slow*, Farrar, Straus and Giroux, New York, 2013.

For the responses to *Remote Footbridge* as compared with *Footbridge*, see Joshua D. Greene et al., 'Pushing Moral Buttons: The Interaction between Personal Force and Intention in Moral Judgment', *Cognition*, 111 (2009), pp. 364–71.

On responses to adult incest, see Jonathan Haidt, 'The Emotional Dog and its Rational Tail', *Psychological Review*, 108/4 (2001), pp. 814–34, and the report of the German Ethics Council *Inzestverbot:Stellungnahme*, 24 September 2014, <http://www.ethikrat.org/publikationen/stellungnahmen/inzestverbot>.

For the relationship between reasoning less and supporting retributive punishment, see 'Beyond Point-and-Shoot Morality', pp. 705–6. Greene cites research by Michael J. Sargent, 'Less Thought, More Punishment: Need for Cognition Predicts Support for Punitive Responses to Crime', *Personality and Social Psychology Bulletin*, 30 (2004), pp. 1485–93.

On wide reflective equilibrium, see Norman Daniels, *Justice and Justification*, Cambridge University Press, Cambridge, 1996. Greene's comment about making things better making moral sense to everyone is on p. 724 of 'Beyond Point-and-Shoot Morality'.

The argument we use to buttress Greene's case for consequentialism is more fully stated in Katarzyna de Lazari-Radek and Peter Singer, *The Point of View of the Universe: Sidgwick and Contemporary Ethics*, Oxford University Press, Oxford, 2014, especially ch. 6. We respond to critics in 'Doing our Best for Hedonistic Utilitarianism: Reply to Critics', *Etica & Politica/Ethics & Politics*, 18 (2016), pp. 187–207.

Chapter 3: What should we maximize?

The classical view

For Aristotle's view of pleasure, see *Nicomachean Ethics*, 1172b26–7. For Plato, see *Gorgias*, 495d–e, 500d. Ancient objections to Epicurean ideas as being worthy of pigs are discussed by David Konstan in 'Epicurean Happiness: A Pig's Life', *Journal of Ancient Philosophy*, 6 (2012), available online at: <http://www.revistas. usp.br/filosofiaantiga/article/download/43309/46932>. Roger Crisp invites us to compare the life of Haydn with that of an immortal oyster in 'Hedonism Reconsidered', *Philosophy and Phenomenological Research*, 73 (2006), pp. 619–45. Mill's claim that it is better to be a dissatisfied human than a satisfied pig is in *Utilitarianism*, ch. 2.

The experience machine

Nozick imagines an 'experience machine' in *Anarchy, State and Utopia*, Basic Books, New York, 1974, p. 43.

Preference utilitarianism

For Peter Singer's previous support for preference utilitarianism, see his *Practical Ethics*, 3rd edn, Cambridge University Press, Cambridge, 2011, p. 14.

Parfit's example of the altruistic drug pusher is from *Reasons and Persons*, Clarendon Press, Oxford, 1984, p. 497. His example of the stranger on the train is from the same book, at p. 151.

We owe to Richard Yetter Chappell the suggestion that instead of switching to fully informed desires, a preference utilitarian could take account of underlying desires.

Rawls's example of the man who desires to count blades of grass is from *A Theory of Justice*, p. 379. The quote from Harsanyi about unreasonable wants is from 'Morality and the Theory of Rational Behaviour', in A. Sen and B. Williams, eds, *Utilitarianism and Beyond*, Cambridge University Press, Cambridge, 1982, p. 55. The point about preference utilitarianism becoming a quite different theory if it takes only reasonable desires into account is made by Shelly Kagan, *Normative Ethics*, Westview, Boulder, Col., 1998, p. 39; Yew-Kwang Ng presses a related argument against Harsanyi in much more detail in his 'Utility, Informed Preference, or Happiness: Following Harsanyi's Argument to its Logical Conclusion', *Social Choice and Welfare*, 16 (1999), pp. 197–216.

Pluralist consequentialism

Parfit, in an appendix to *Reasons and Persons* entitled 'What Makes Someone's Life Go Best', divides theories of what makes someone's life go best into three categories: hedonistic theories, desire-fulfilment theories, and objective list theories. Theories in this latter group hold that 'certain things are good or bad for us, whether or not we want to have the good things, or to avoid the bad things'. Those who support such a theory and hold that there are intrinsic values other than happiness or pleasure are, in our terminology, pluralist consequentialists who regard some things of intrinsic value as part of our well-being, even if they do not contribute to our happiness or pleasure, or satisfy our desires.

Mill is presented as a supporter of the intrinsic value of freedom in Prasanta Pattanaik and Yongsheng Xu, 'Freedom and its Value', in Iwao Hirose and Jonas Olson, eds, *The Oxford Handbook of Value Theory*, Oxford University Press, Oxford, 2015.

The list of goods that philosophers have held to be of intrinsic value draws on: William Frankena, *Ethics*, 2nd edn, Prentice-Hall, Englewood Cliffs, NJ, 1973, pp. 87–8, available at <http://www.ditext.com/frankena/ethics.html>; John Finnis, *Natural Law and Natural Rights*, 2nd edn, Oxford University Press, Oxford, 1982; and Timothy Chappell, *Understanding Human Goods*, Edinburgh University Press, Edinburgh, 1998, ch. 4.

Value beyond sentient beings

For Moore's changing views, see *Principia Ethica*, Cambridge University Press, Cambridge, 1903, pp. 135–6 and his *Ethics*, Williams & Norgate, London, 1912, pp. 103–4, 148, 153.

Intrinsic value: the story so far

The preference for the lottery ticket you choose is taken from Ellen Langer, 'The Illusion of Control', *Journal of Personality and Social Psychology*, 32 (1975), pp. 311–28, and for the belief that an accident is less likely if one is driving, see Frank McKenna, 'It Won't Happen to Me: Unrealistic Optimism or Illusion of Control', *British Journal of Psychology*, 84 (1993), pp. 39–50. The quote from Lefcourt is from 'The Functions of the Illusions of Control and Freedom', *American Psychologist*, 28 (1973), p. 424.

For the experiments indicating that people would be reluctant to leave the life they are leading, whether it is real or an illusion, see F. De Brigard, 'If you Like it, Does it Matter if it's Real?', *Philosophical Psychology*, 23 (2010), pp. 43–57.

What is pleasure?

Roger Crisp defends the 'feeling tone' view in 'Hedonism
Reconsidered', *Philosophy and Phenomenological Research*,
73 (2006), pp. 619–45, and in *Reason and the Good*, Clarendon
Press, Oxford, 2006, pp. 103–11. For the experiment in which
electrodes were implanted in the brains of rats, see J. Olds and
P. Milner, 'Positive Reinforcement Produced by Electrical
Stimulation of Septal Area and Other Regions of Rat Brain',
Journal of Comparative and Physiological Psychology, 47
(1954), pp. 419–27. For the view that pleasure is a 'niceness
gloss', see Morten Kringelbach and Kent Berridge, eds,
Pleasures of the Brain, Oxford University Press, Oxford,
2009, p. 9.

For the view that happiness is a disposition to be in a good mood, and
so on, see Daniel Haybron, *The Pursuit of Unhappiness*, Oxford
University Press, Oxford, 2008. For a different perspective on
happiness see Fred Feldman, *What is This Thing Called
Happiness*, Oxford University Press, Oxford, 2012.

Chapter 4: Objections

For critical discussion of utilitarianism, see J. J. C. Smart and Bernard
Williams, *Utilitarianism For & Against*, Cambridge University
Press, Cambridge, 1973; Amartya Sen and Bernard Williams, eds,
Utilitarianism and Beyond, Cambridge University Press,
Cambridge, 1982; Samuel Scheffler, ed., *Consequentialism and its
Critics*, Oxford University Press, Oxford, 1988; and Samuel
Scheffler, *The Rejection of Consequentialism*, Clarendon Press,
Oxford, 1994.

Does utilitarianism tell us to act immorally?

Ivan's challenge is to be found in Fyodor Dostoevsky, *The Brothers
Karamazov*, trans. Ignat Avsey, Oxford University Press, Oxford,
1994, pt 2, bk 5, ch. 4. The example of the sheriff and the lynch
mob is from H. J. McCloskey, 'An Examination of Restricted
Utilitarianism', *Philosophical Review*, 66 (1957), pp. 466–85; repr.
in Michael D. Bayles, ed., *Contemporary Utilitarianism*, Peter
Smith, Gloucester, Mass., 1978, where the example is on p. 121.
The quote from Elizabeth Anscombe is from 'Modern Moral
Philosophy', *Philosophy*, 33 (1958), p. 17.

Measuring utility

Edgeworth proposes his method of measuring utility in his
*Mathematical Psychics: An Essay on the Application of
Mathematics to the Moral Sciences*, C. Kegan Paul, London, 1881,
appendix III, 'On Hedonimetry', pp. 98–102.

For an outline of the use of Quality-Adjusted Life-Years as a measure
of health benefits, see Milton C. Weinstein, George Torrance,
and Alistair McGuire, 'QALYs: The Basics', *Value in Health*, 12
(2009), Supplement 1, pp. S5–S9, and for a fuller discussion of the
ethics of this approach, see John McKie, Jeff Richardson, Peter
Singer, and Helga Kuhse, *The Allocation of Health Care Resources:
An Ethical Evaluation of the 'QALY' Approach*, Ashgate, Aldershot,
1998. For the work of the National Institute for Health and Care
Excellence, see <http://www.nice.org.uk>.

For an overview of the state of brain science relative to pleasure and
happiness, see Moren Kringelbach and Kent Berridge, 'The
Neuroscience of Happiness and Pleasure', *Social Research*, 77
(2010), pp. 659–78.

Bentham writes about not expecting exact measurement in *Introduction
to the Principles of Morals and Legislation*, ch. 4, para. 15.

Is utilitarianism too demanding?

The insight that 'What ought we to do?' and 'What ought we to praise
and blame people for doing?' are different questions comes
from Sidgwick, *The Methods of Ethics*, p. 493. Norcross proposes
scalar utilitarianism in Alastair Norcross, 'The Scalar Approach
to Utilitarianism', in H. West, ed., *Blackwell Guide to Mill's
Utilitarianism*, Blackwell, Oxford, 2006, pp. 217–32. On
demandingness more generally, see de Lazari-Radek and Singer,
The Point of View of the Universe, pp. 317–36.

Does utilitarianism ignore our special obligations?

William Godwin wrote about rescuing Archbishop Fénelon rather
than his own mother in *An Enquiry Concerning Political Justice
and its Influence on General Virtue and Happiness*, Knopf, New
York, 1926 (first published 1793), pp. 41–2. He presents a more
sympathetic view of partial relationships in *Memoirs of the Author
of a Vindication of the Rights of Woman*, ch. vi, p. 90, 2nd edn, as
quoted in William Godwin, *Thoughts Occasioned by the Perusal of
Dr Parr's Spital Sermon*, Taylor and Wilks, London, 1801; repr. in
J. Marken and B. Pollin, eds, *Uncollected Writings (1785–1822) by*

William Godwin, Scholars' Facsimiles and Reprints, Gainesville, Fla., 1968, pp. 314–15.

Parfit's discussion of 'blameless wrongdoing' is in *Reasons and Persons*, ch. 1, sect. 14.

Our account of Paul Farmer is from Tracy Kidder, *Mountains Beyond Mountains*, Random House, New York, 2003.

Ignoring 'the separateness of persons'

The standard reference for this objection is John Rawls, *A Theory of Justice*, pp. 20–4. Rawls was not, however, the first to make this point; that honour appears to go to David Gauthier, *Practical Reasoning*, Clarendon Press, Oxford, 1963, pp. 123–7.

The interpretation of the separateness of persons objection as directed against the idea that individuals are mere receptacles comes from Richard Yetter Chappell, 'Value Receptacles', *Noûs*, 49 (2015), pp. 322–32.

For a critical examination of Kant's objection to using someone as a means, see Parfit, *On What Matters*, vol. 1, ch. 9. In this chapter Parfit gives several examples of the justifiable use of someone as a means. Our example is closest to his *Third Earthquake*, on p. 222.

The distribution of utility

The standard reference for prioritarianism is Parfit, *Equality or Priority? (The Lindley Lecture, 1991)*, University of Kansas, Lawrence, Kan., 1991; a shorter version was published as 'Equality and Priority' in *Ratio*, 10 (1997), pp. 202–21. Other discussions include: Richard Arneson, 'Luck Egalitarianism and Prioritarianism', *Ethics*, 110 (2000), pp. 339–49; Roger Crisp, 'Equality, Priority and Compassion', *Ethics*, 113 (2003), pp. 745–63; Larry Temkin, 'Equality, Priority, or What?', *Economics and Philosophy*, 19 (2003), pp. 61–87; and Toby Ord, 'A New Counterexample to Prioritarianism', *Utilitas*, 27 (2015), pp. 298–302.

On normative uncertainty, see William MacAskill, Krister Bykvist, and Toby Ord, *Moral Uncertainty*, Oxford University Press, Oxford (forthcoming).

Chapter 5: Rules

Two forms of utilitarianism

The 'overwhelming majority' criterion is taken from Brad Hooker, *Ideal Code, Real World*, Clarendon Press, Oxford, 2000, p. 80. An influential early article defending rule-utilitarianism is Richard Brandt, 'Toward a Credible Form of Utilitarianism', in H.-N. Castañeda and G. Nakhnikian, eds, *Morality and the Language of Conduct*, Wayne State University Press, Detroit, 1963, pp. 107–43. Also influential was J. O. Urmson's argument that Mill was a rule-utilitarian, in 'The Interpretation of the Moral Philosophy of J. S. Mill', *Philosophical Quarterly*, 10 (1953), pp. 33–9. Smart's 'rule-worship' objection to rule-utilitarianism is in 'Extreme and Restricted Utilitarianism', *Philosophical Quarterly*, 6 (1956), pp. 344–54, at p. 348–9. The objection that some forms of rule-utilitarianism collapse into act-utilitarianism comes from David Lyons, *Forms and Limits of Utilitarianism*, Oxford University Press, Oxford, 1965.

The ticking bomb

For the ticking bomb scenario in fiction, see 'Ticking time bomb scenario', <https://en.wikipedia.org/wiki/Ticking_time_bomb_scenario>. The United Nations Convention Against Torture is available at <http://www.un.org/documents/ga/res/39/a39r046.htm>.

Keeping it secret

Sidgwick's reluctant acceptance of esoteric morality is in *The Methods of Ethics*, pp. 489–90. Bernard Williams criticizes it in *Ethics and the Limits of Philosophy*, Fontana, London, 1985, p. 108.

Is utilitarianism self-effacing?

The distinction between whether a theory is self-effacing and whether it is true was made by Parfit, *Reasons and Persons*, ch. 1, sect. 17. Bentham's response to the allegation that the principle of utility is a dangerous principle comes from a footnote to his *Introduction to the Principles of Morals and Legislation*, ch. 1, para. 13. Also relevant to this section is Richard Yetter Chappell, 'What's wrong with self-effacing theories?', *Philosophy, et cetera*, 16 November 2008, <http://www.philosophyetc.net/2008/11/whats-wrong-with-self-effacing-theories.html>.

Chapter 6: Utilitarianism in action

Applying utilitarianism today

Stuart Hampshire's suggestion that utilitarianism had ceased to be bold was made in 'Morality and Pessimism', the Leslie Stephen

Lecture delivered at the University of Cambridge in 1972 and repr. in Stuart Hampshire, *Public and Private Morality*, Cambridge University Press, Cambridge, 1978. We owe the quote to Robert Goodin, *Utilitarianism as a Public Philosophy*, Cambridge University Press, Cambridge, 1995, p. 3.

End of life decisions

The full decision of Justice Lynn Smith in *Carter v Canada* can be found here: <https://bccla.org/wp-content/uploads/2012/06/Carter-v-Canada-AG-2012-BCSC-886.pdf>.

Jocelyn Downie gives a brief account of the decision of the Supreme Court of Canada at: <https://impactethics.ca/2015/02/11/in-a-nutshell-the-supreme-court-of-canada-decision-in-carter-v-canada-attorney-general/>.

For a utilitarian approach to end of life decisions, see Peter Singer, *Rethinking Life and Death*, Oxford University Press, Oxford, 1995.

Ethics and animals

For a utilitarian approach to the ethics of our relationship with animals, including descriptions of factory farming and research on animals, see Peter Singer, *Animal Liberation*, Harper Perennial, New York, 2002 (first published 1975). Bentham's famous footnote insisting that the key question is whether animals can suffer is in his *Introduction to the Principles of Morals and Legislation*, ch. 17, sect. 1. On the capacity of animals, including fish, to experience pleasure and pain and much else besides, see Jonathan Balcombe, *Second Nature*, St Martin's Griffin, New York, 2011, and the same author's *What a Fish Knows*, Scientific American/Farrar, Straus and Giroux, New York, 2016. Peter Godfrey-Smith's *Other Minds: The Octopus, the Sea and the Deep Origins of Consciousness*, Farrar, Straus and Giroux, New York, 2016, discusses evidence for the intelligence and consciousness of an invertebrate animal. Mill showed his willingness to stake the validity of utilitarianism on the question of concern for animal suffering in 'Whewell on Moral Philosophy', first published 1852, repr. in J. S. Mill, *Collected Works*, vol. 10, University of Toronto Press and Routledge & Kegan Paul, Toronto and London, 1985.

Bentham's defence of killing animals is from the previously cited passage in *Introduction to the Principles of Morals and Legislation*, ch. 17, sect. 1. For the contemporary continuation of this debate, see Peter Singer and Jim Mason, *The Ethics of What We Eat*,

Rodale, New York, 2006, pp. 249ff.; Peter Singer, *Practical Ethics*, ch. 5; Tatjana Višak, *Killing Happy Animals*, Palgrave Macmillan, London, 2013; and Tatjana Višak and Robert Garner, eds, *The Ethics of Killing Animals*, Oxford University Press, Oxford, 2016.

Effective altruism

Bentham argued for relief for the poor, at public expense, in *Principles of the Civil Code* and in *Writings on the Poor Laws*. His most explicit statement that the needs of the poor should outweigh the rights of the rich to superfluity is in *Principles of the Civil Code*, in John Bowring, ed., *The Works of Jeremy Bentham*, William Tait, Edinburgh, 1843, vol. 1, republished by Liberty Fund, <http://oll. libertyfund.org/titles/bentham-the-works-of-jeremy-bentham-vol-1>; see especially p. 314. We owe this reference to Michael Quinn, 'Mill on Population, Poverty and Poor Relief: Out of Bentham by Malthus?', *Revue d'études benthamiennes*, 4 (2008), available online: <https://etudes-benthamiennes.revues. org/185#ftn48>.

On the decline in the number of people in extreme poverty, see World Bank, 'Poverty Overview', <http://www.worldbank.org/en/topic/ poverty/overview>. For child mortality, see the reports of UNICEF, available at <https://www.unicef.org/reports>.

Peter Singer's 'Famine, Affluence and Morality' is available with other related essays in *Famine, Affluence and Morality*, Oxford University Press, Oxford, 2016; for a fuller utilitarian discussion of the obligations of the affluent in regard to global poverty, see Peter Singer, *The Life You Can Save*, Random House, New York, 2009. Nick Bostrom argues for the importance of existential risk in 'Existential Risk Management as Global Priority', *Global Policy*, 4 (2013), pp. 15–31.

Key books on effective altruism include Will MacAskill, *Doing Good Better*, Gotham, New York, 2015; Peter Singer, *The Most Good You Can Do*, Yale University Press, New Haven, 2015; and Ryan Carey, ed., *The Effective Altruism Handbook*, Centre for Effective Altruism, 2015, available from <http://www.careyryan.com/files/ EA_Handbook.pdf>.

The survey of effective altruists showing that the majority are utilitarian is 'The 2015 Survey of Effective Altruists: Results and Analysis', posted by Chris Cundy for the Effective Altruism Forum's impact team, and available at <http://effective-altruism.com/ea/ zw/the_2015_survey_of_effective_altruists_results/>.

The striking differences in value obtained by different approaches to aid for people in need are outlined by Toby Ord in 'The moral imperative towards cost-effectiveness in global health', Centre for Global Development, Washington, DC, 2013, available at <www.cgdev.org/content/publications/detail/1427016>.

Population puzzles

Sidgwick raised the choice between the average and total views in *The Methods of Ethics*, pp. 414–16. The most influential presentation of the problem is in Parfit, *Reasons and Persons*, part IV. A useful recent discussion is Gustaf Arrhenius, Jesper Ryberg, and Torbjörn Tännsjö, 'The Repugnant Conclusion', in *The Stanford Encyclopedia of Philosophy*, available at <www.plato.stanford.edu/archives/spr2014/entries/repugnant-conclusion>.

Gross national happiness

World Happiness Reports are available at <http://worldhappiness.report>. Guidelines on measuring subjective well-being from the Organization for Economic Cooperation and Development are: *OECD Guidelines on Measuring Subjective Well-being*, OECD Publishing, 2013, <http://dx.doi.org/10.1787/9789264191655-en>.

Index

SOCIAL MEDIA
Very Short Introduction

Join our community

www.oup.com/vsi

- Join us online at the official Very Short Introductions **Facebook** page.
- Access the thoughts and musings of our authors with our online **blog**.
- Sign up for our monthly **e-newsletter** to receive information on all new titles publishing that month.
- Browse the full range of Very Short Introductions online.
- Read **extracts** from the Introductions for free.
- If you are a teacher or lecturer you can order inspection copies quickly and simply via our website.

ONLINE
CATALOGUE
A Very Short Introduction

Our online catalogue is designed to make it easy to find your
ideal Very Short Introduction. View the entire collection by subject
area, watch author videos, read sample chapters, and download
reading guides.

http://global.oup.com/uk/academic/general/vsi_list/

GERMAN
PHILOSOPHY
A Very Short Introduction
Andrew Bowie

German Philosophy: A Very Short Introduction discusses the
idea that German philosophy forms one of the most revealing
responses to the problems of 'modernity'. The rise of the modern
natural sciences and the related decline of religion raises a
series of questions, which recur throughout German philosophy,
concerning the relationships between knowledge and faith,
reason and emotion, and scientific, ethical, and artistic ways
of seeing the world. There are also many significant philosophers
who are generally neglected in most existing English-language
treatments of German philosophy, which tend to concentrate
on the canonical figures. This *Very Short Introduction* will include
reference to these thinkers and suggests how they can be
used to question more familiar German philosophical thought.

BEAUTY
A Very Short Introduction
Roger Scruton

In this *Very Short Introduction* the renowned philosopher Roger Scruton explores the concept of beauty, asking what makes an object - either in art, in nature, or the human form - beautiful, and examining how we can compare differing judgements of beauty when it is evident all around us that our tastes vary so widely. Is there a right judgement to be made about beauty? Is it right to say there is more beauty in a classical temple than a concrete office block, more in a Rembrandt than in last year's Turner Prize winner? Forthright and thought-provoking, and as accessible as it is intellectually rigorous, this introduction to the philosophy of beauty draws conclusions that some may find controversial, but, as Scruton shows, help us to find greater sense of meaning in the beautiful objects that fill our lives.

A fascinating book, which I heartily recommend.

Brya Wilson, Readers Digest